Talk about Poetry

By the Same Author

Poetry

The Benefit Forms
Going Out to Vote
Overdrawn Account
Anaglypta
This Other Life
More about the Weather
Entertaining Fates
Leaf-viewing
Lost and Found
Via Sauro Variations
Anywhere You Like
About Time Too
Selected Poems
There are Avenues
Ghost Characters

Prose

Untitled Deeds

Translations

Six Poems by Ungaretti
The Great Friend and Other Translated Poems
The Greener Meadow: Selected Poems of Luciano Erba
Selected Poetry and Prose of Vittorio Sereni

Criticism

In the Circumstances: About Poems and Poets
Poetry, Poets, Readers: Making Things Happen
Twentieth Century Poetry: Selves and Situations

PETER ROBINSON

TALK ABOUT POETRY
conversations on the art

Shearsman Books
Exeter

Published in the United Kingdom in 2007 by
Shearsman Books Ltd
58 Velwell Road
Exeter EX4 4LD

ISBN-13 978-1-905700-04-2   //   ISBN-10 1-905700-04-0

Acknowledgements
The first conversation, with Ted Slade, appeared in *The Poetry Kit* in 1999; the second, with Ian Sansom, in *Oxford Poetry* in 1994; the third and fourth, with Marcus Perryman, in *The Animist* and *The Cortland Review* in 1998. The fifth, with Nate Dorward, appeared in *Jacket* in 2002. The seventh, with Peter Carpenter, was published in *Poetry Ireland Review* in 2004. The eighth, with Katy Price, appeared in *Salt* in 2003. The ninth, with Adam Piette, partly appeared in *Tears in the Fence* in 2003; the tenth, with Alex Pestell, appeared in the magazine *Signals* in 2005; the last formed the basis for a profile by Tom Phillips published in *The Venue* in February 2006. With the exception of the interview with Ian Sansom, done by airmail, and the one with Jane Davies, which was tape-recorded, transcribed and revised, the texts were produced by electronic exchanges followed by mutually agreed revisions. The collaborative help of the interviewers is warmly and gratefully acknowledged, as is that of the journal editors where these conversations first appeared. Nor, finally, should the sustained support of my wife and children go without mention here.

The publisher gratefully acknowledges financial assistance from
Arts Council England.

Preface

This book developed piece-meal over the decade following Ian Sansom's suggestion that we do an interview for the magazine he was helping to edit. It began to take on shape and some coherence during the conversations with Marcus Perryman. As interconnected questions about poetry, its composition, publication, and reception were received and responded to, the possibility of a sequence of dialogues began to evolve. The questions asked were frequently also about the life of a contemporary poet, a life that has included a fairly representative measure of happiness and sorrow, belonging and displacement, success and neglect, achievement, failure, and continuity of effort. One of the things that made such a life possible has been the support of the friends and colleagues with whom these conversations were conducted. Nor is it a coincidence that the interviews making up these chapters were, with just two exceptions, conducted entirely at long distance and by e-mail.

The benefits of electronic mail, especially for those who in another age might have been described as in exile, are hard to underestimate. Despite the virtual condition of the messages, and the difficulties of tone and address to be accommodated, it's surely evident that this form of rapid communication has helped create the possibility for worldwide support networks and collaborative communities. Poets have immemorially tended to be sustained letter-writers. This mode of communication has simply made it more convenient for them to keep up their massive correspondences. Entirely unforeseeably, in 1989, at the age of thirty-six, I stopped living in the country of my birth. For me, e-mail arrived some five or six years later; it dramatically reduced the sense of isolation and exclusion that I had come to feel was an inevitable consequence of that mid-life change of place.

Naturally enough, much of what follows is concerned with the corner of the vast poetry endeavour that is represented by my writings. Nevertheless, as is made clear by the very first exchanges in the first interview, however isolated the individuals concerned, culture cannot take place in an imaginative vacuum. The following dialogues about the life and art of poetry are the results of more than three decades of reading or writing, and of innumerable conversations with poets from various countries and cultures. The replies presented are of course my ideas about poetry and matters related to it; but there is also simultaneously a representation of the kinds of prompted thoughts it was possible to have with others at this point in the evolution of the art.

In the course of separate conversations with different people, there was naturally the need to fill in some similar information so as to provide context for questions about different issues. While some slight cuts have been done to remove repetitions, I hope readers will understand the ways in which issues are necessarily returned to here and there. These eleven interviews were conducted over a period of as many years, busy years in which I remarried and became a father, years which saw the end of the millennium and what seems like a change of era. The person who began talking to Ian Sansom in 1994 was at a distinctly different stage of life from the one adding a few sentences to this preface. There will inevitably be changes of emphasis in the responses to questions that follow. There may well be some self-contradiction. Rather than go back over everything artificially constructing a coherent position that none of the versions of me ever held, I thought it best to let the exchanges stand more or less as previously published.

I hope readers, writers, and students of poetry will benefit from what follows — and as much from inner debate or promptings to respond differently as from agreement with what I say, or, indeed, the acknowledgement that such things might have needed, and been worth, saying.

Peter Robinson
18 February 2006

Contents

ONE

Tell me about your background

TED SLADE: *Where were you born and brought up?*

I'm a vicar's son born in 1953 and brought up in a series of poor, urban parishes in the industrial north west of England. My birthplace is Salford, Lancashire, but with the exception of five years between the ages of 9 and 14 spent in Wigan, I grew up in Bootle and Garston, two different parts of Liverpool. My parents still live in the south of the city, and I think of it as my hometown. In 1996 I edited an anthology, *Liverpool Accents: Seven Poets and a City*, as a form of homage to the place.

Do you come from a literary family?

No. My parents are the first members of their respective families, and the only members of their generations, to go to university. They met at Durham in the immediate post-war years; my mother was there studying geography and my dad had discovered a vocation for the ministry in Bedford in 1942 while training for a modest role in the Intelligence Corps at Bletchley Park. There were a few poetry books and anthologies in the house. I don't think they'd been looked at for quite a number of years when I started rifling through them in the second half of the 1960s. However, I do come from a fairly cultured and artistic family: my mother's parents played duets on piano and violin (come to think of it, they had a complete set of the works of Lawrence locked in a glass-fronted bookcase); my maternal grandfather was a serious amateur photographer; one of my mother's sisters went to Art School; my parents sang madrigals at one point, and are still involved with the performance of Church music. I was singing poems by William Blake and George Herbert and William Cowper before I knew what they were.

That seems pretty 'literary' to me . . .

Yes, perhaps it was, in comparison to what I read of Tony Harrison's childhood, for instance; but aside from a great-aunt who privately printed a collection of children's stories, to my knowledge I'm the family's only published author (though one of my brothers has co-edited a collection of papers on his research field in Physics). Mum reads novels; dad reads the papers. All I'm saying is that I'm not Gert Hofmann's son, or Roy Fuller's.

Did your poetry come directly out of that environment, or were there other influences that set you off?

That environment involved moving around a lot in my childhood. The poem 'On Van Gogh's *La Crau*' in *Entertaining Fates* has these house removals in it. I changed places at the ages of approximately less-than-one, three, nine, fourteen, eighteen, and twenty-one . . . It crossed my mind recently that I've lived in the same flat in Sendai, Japan, for eight years now — and that's longer than in any other single place, including all my thirty-six years of residence in England or Wales. I tend to think that the moving around we did when I was young produced a sense of protective detachment from situations that may have helped to stimulate a poet's stance towards the world. Yet I don't believe my brother, less than two years younger, did the same; or he found a different way of managing childhood insecurities.

Vicarage children have a built-in sense that they don't quite belong: they get told it by the kids from the local church school, and if they are growing up in poor parishes, then there may well be wildly discrepant assumptions of class and cultural difference in the mix too. In Wigan I discovered that my schoolmates came, by and large, from extended mining families with networks of relatives living sometimes in the same street. We were an emphatically nuclear family: my parents weren't in close touch with their siblings, and the surviving grandparents were in what seemed very distant towns. I wrote about some of this in 'Liverpool . . . of all places', my piece of autobiographical prose in the *Liverpool Accents* anthology.

One more thought on this would be that you can mention any bit of autobiography you like, and other people can be found who experienced the same things (my nearest brother, for instance) or more acute forms of them, and they didn't turn into writers — so the biographical facts might be necessary to explain why I did, but they can't be sufficient.

What sort of poetry did you begin writing — what were its main themes and techniques?

Between 1969 and 1974, when I graduated from York University, I wrote reams of poems in a variety of styles, imitating whatever I was reading or studying. The poetry I started writing was about my paternal grandfather (who died when I was five), landscapes of Liverpool and the Yorkshire Dales, the circumstances of my childhood and youth, girl trouble, student radicalism and Northern Ireland, paintings by Rembrandt ... and it tended to be in patterned but usually irregular metres with varying degrees of rhyme — from full to hardly any at all. Though I like to think I've got better at what I do, the non-aligned formal eclecticism I picked up as a student writer has stayed with me.

How did you first get your poems published?

My first published poem (a pastiche ballad) was in an anthology made on a hand press the school had acquired; another appeared in a mimeographed sixth-form magazine. I was involved in publishing two pamphlets with a student poet called Hugh Macpherson at York, and also appeared regularly in issues of the student magazines. At Cambridge in 1976, I started to edit with a series of co-editors, the magazine *Perfect Bound,* and early poems that I've reprinted went in there. By this stage I had started sending off to little magazines, and towards the end of the 1970s began to appear in the likes of *Stand*, in the *New Poetry* anthologies, and a couple of times on the BBC's *Poetry Now* programme. My first separate publications were *The Benefit Forms*, a pamphlet published by Richard Tabor with a grant from the Eastern Arts Association, and *Going Out to Vote*, a broadsheet done by John Welch's Many Press, both in 1978. By this stage I thought of myself as up and running; but it would be another decade before a book came out from one of the larger specialist presses, Carcanet. Looking back, it seems to me a standard 'paying your dues' kind of apprenticeship in the days before the big competitions and the leaps to public notice of the 1980s.

How did this breakthrough to a collection come about?

I'm not sure about a breakthrough . . . I can clearly recall offering manuscripts to Anvil and Bloodaxe in the very early 1980s, not long after a first book with a spine, *Overdrawn Account* (1980) from the Many Press had garnered a surprisingly large number of reasonable reviews. In both cases I got the usual reply. At which point, I seem to have gone into hibernation, emerging in 1985 with a pamphlet (also from the Many Press) called *Anaglypta*. This came out at the same time as the Cambridge Poetry Festival of that year, a big event with a performance of Ezra Pound's opera, *Villon*, and a tie-in exhibition at the Tate Gallery (I did one of the essays for the catalogue) on the 100th anniversary of his birth. I was the chairman of the organizing committee. Anyway, I think it was at this festival that Peter Jay talked about doing a selection of Vittorio Sereni's poems, and Michael Schmidt (who'd published some things in *PN Review*) said, in passing, something like: 'You must send me a manuscript …' The former took five years to come out, the latter three.

How was it received, critically, and by buyers? How did that influence your writing?

Well, *This Other Life* did surprisingly well: it was positively reviewed in most of the big places. Martin Dodsworth gave the book a very positive description in *The Guardian*, where I was paired with Les Murray. He was asked to nominate the Cheltenham Prize in the same year, and generously gave it to that book. I did a host of readings, was paired with Jo Shapcott in the New Voices series at the South Bank, and did three radio broadcasts. The book had sold out some time early in the next decade. I don't know the exact print run, but it can't have been that large.

I'm not sure that it was only this little bit of recognition that had an equivocal effect on my work (I was going into the phase that would precipitate me out of the British Isles and my first marriage); but a sense that I must be doing something right and that therefore people would be interested in what I produced led to some self-critical slackness that slightly weakens the next, rather too long book, *Entertaining Fates* (1992) — which, mysteriously, received only one review and that a nasty one in the Carcanet-connected journal *PN Review*. My own sense, and that of reviewers or people who've written to me, seems to be that with the chapbook *Leaf-viewing* (1992) and the collection *Lost and Found* (1997) I hit a surer vein.

You were involved in some of the developments in the '80s that led to poetry being described briefly as 'the new rock and roll'. Can you say something about that involvement? What lasting effects do you think what was done then has had on the readership for poetry?

It was all part of 'paying my dues': I arrived in Cambridge in the autumn of 1975 and found that there had been a large poetry festival (organized by Richard Burns) the previous spring. The organizer for 1977 had decided to concentrate on the avant-garde poets of Cambridge, London, Europe and America. I was made the secretary of the organizing committee, and learned a lot. This event was something like a luxurious poet's conference: money being spent lavishly on travel, hospitality, and the elegant festival programme, while the tasks of getting an audience to pay the bills were neglected. The inevitable result was that the society ended up deep in debt. At this point I took it over, went for a pluralistic approach, found a brilliant treasurer and colleague in the person of Alison Rimmer (as she then was), a director of Heffers Bookshop. With the 1979 festival, we got the society back into the black and put together a programme that could include a Sound/Performance poetry day, a debate on poetry and politics between Jon Silkin and Donald Davie, and readings by such poets as C. H. Sisson, Josef Brodsky, Anne Waldman and Allen Ginsberg. In fact, it was Ginsberg who helped us most with our debt problem: he did a sell-out Saturday night performance with Peter Orlovsky and a guitarist for the price of one-way air tickets (he was finessing a European tour) and £50 each.

That was my main contribution: after a break, I helped organize some Italian events in 1983 and oversaw the proceedings in 1985. It was on the basis of this expertise that Maura Dooley asked me to work part-time as an advisor for the 1988 Poetry International at the South Bank Centre. Preparing for it on a weekly and then daily basis with her was a great pleasure, but those kinds of events take their toll in stress — and the feeling of emptiness that came over me when it had finished contributed to a growing mood of quiet desperation that drove me to accept what I thought was a stop-gap job-offer to teach for a couple of years in Kyoto.

The lasting effects of poetry's public promotion as a Cinderella of the entertainment industry are probably mixed. There's the dumbing-down side (if it can't 'connect', like a stand-up comic's work, then it can get lost) and there's the access side — you may get exposed to great art being delivered by the people who made it, even if you only went along for a laugh.

Living and working in provincial Japan is obviously quite a contrast from your original background. How has this move influenced your work?

I've been asked about this a number of times at readings and in other interviews. The first thing to say is that I came to Japan because I hadn't found regular employment in England and was offered that two-year temporary job at Kyoto University, so took it as a break from a situation grim-ish on various counts in 1989. After being here about a year, I was offered a job with an annually renewable contract at Tohoku University in Sendai — and, aside from almost a year away to have and recover from a brain tumour operation, I've been here ever since. This has happened by taking one decision at a time, and was in no sense foreseen. I didn't come to Japan because I'm interested in Zen and archery, ukiyoe, haiku, or ikebana . . . To me, it's the place where I earn a living, and, somewhat to my surprise, I've started to feel that I know my way around — as well as learning something about Japanese arts and crafts into the bargain.

You call it provincial Japan, and that's right; it's not Tokyo, a place I don't much enjoy visiting, and is treated as distinctly 'hick' in Japanese culture. When Shakespeare's plays are translated, it's conventional practice to render the speeches of the rude mechanicals into the local dialect. However, Sendai is a city with a population of over a million: that's larger than any of the places I was brought up in — places with local accents that figure in the cultural mythology of Britain somewhat similarly.

The poems I write have inevitably been dramatically shaped by this largely unplanned change of life. The phrase 'jet lag and birdsong' in 'Their Fears' from Lost and Found, for example, would not have come to my pen before I started a love-hate relationship with the Boeing 747. Poems, for me, come out of the circumstances of life, and since so much of my life takes place in Japanese circumstances, some of the details of the place have naturally rubbed off. However, I've tried to keep away from tourist poems, or Japan-explaining poems — though there have been inevitable lapses. I've just hoped more or less to continue doing what I used to do but in different places.

The great advantage of 'exile' for a writer, or, more strictly in my case, economic migration, is that you are freed at a stroke from the innumerable ways in which a native culture sets the agenda and delineates the pale of thought and feeling. It does this so thoroughly that it's only when you've got clear of it that you begin to see how much you've been shaped. Perhaps the greatest supposed danger is that you lose touch with your native tongue. Frankly, I think that's a parochial anxiety. I teach Literature in English, and English as a Second Language. I watch the different European and American news broadcasts by satellite at breakfast each morning. I'm in e-mail, fax, and phone contact with relatives, friends, and colleagues in most of the English-speaking countries and Europe. We live in the fragmentary, poly-lingual foreign community here, where the native Englishes are as likely to be American, Canadian, Australian, or New Zealander as the various UK versions. My wife is an Italian and my elder daughter goes to the local kindergarten, so the family conducts itself in three languages. I have a full-time relationship with a vast Babel of words, both native and foreign, written and spoken. Now I begin get the point of *Finnegans Wake*; sometimes I think I'm living in it . . . It's not that my language has been impoverished by emigration; it's been vastly enlarged.

Can you describe your most effective working method? Do you wait for inspiration, or sit down every day with the intention of writing?

I do both. Translations have to be done on a craft basis. So does fictional prose, so do critical essays — and interviews. Poems have to insist that they need to be written. So I carry around little notebooks, and jot down phrases, titles, and the like when they come to me, and then, if there's a need, I will find the time to bring them to a conclusion. I try to write as little poetry as possible: I don't enjoy the assembly-line feeling, and tend to think that over-production is bad for what I may be able to do.

How important to you are formal workshops, or getting the opinions of other poets about your work-in-progress?

I live in almost complete isolation from other writers here in Japan. I don't attend, or give, formal workshops. I don't think that other poets are always the best people to give advice because they have their own art to keep an eye on, so their comments are naturally shaped by their own way of doing things. When I send copies of poems or books to other poets, and occasionally critics, they tend to be warmly supportive or silent. However, I do show poems to some close and candid friends who are not poets, but are literary people, and I frequently withhold or revise poems on advice from anyone, poet or not. I also send them off to magazines and use the experience of rejection as a way of having second thoughts.

To what extent if any do you collaborate with other artists?

Hardly at all. I'm sure I'd enjoy working with film makers, visual artists, having poems set to music, or doing an opera libretto — but no one's asked me and I can't go looking for the work. I was once involved in the publication of a poem-card: but then I was the visual artist. I've usually enjoyed collaborating on translating poems and editing books or magazines.

Translation is itself a kind of cooperation, I suppose. How do you approach translating poetry? Have you had a chance to work with the original writers?

When I first started working on Italian poetry with Marcus Perryman I hardly knew the language, but wanted to learn it, and so he provided some prose cribs or rough drafts to work up with an eye on the original. That was in 1979. Two decades later, as I say, my wife is Italian and my parents-in-law don't speak English, so I'm more or less able to set the translation going myself and then ask for comments, corrections, and advice.

I've had the experience of collaborating with three living poets, though time has gone by and two of them are now dead. Back in the late 1970s, I did a translation of Alain Delahaye's *L'être perdu* and got in touch with him. We met in Cambridge and worked on the poems together, and he sent me sets of revisions and corrections — to the point where I began to feel, rightly or wrongly, that he was taking over the translations and robbing them of whatever Anglo-Saxon vigour I could impart. When I wrote politely agreeing to differ on a few choices of words, the collaboration came to a sudden end — and the versions have remained unpublished. I still have the drafts and the correspondence.

Discussing translations of his work with the Italian poet Franco Fortini involved listening to him give extended accounts of the implications in the tiniest points, implications that it would have been all but impossible to have conveyed by means of a single English word into a culture where the contexts are not shared. It was, nevertheless, mostly an illuminating experience to sit and listen. Vittorio Sereni was quite different: he was simply supportive of the work, willing to discuss specific details only in terms of what was strictly needed to translate the passage. Sereni believed, I think, that his poems would communicate if you simply translated the most literal and obvious meaning, and then made a coherent poetic form in the second language. Working on his poems brought us into contact with all the stubborn difficulties implied in saying you want to do an accurate rendering that is also a poem in its own right. Some people like to think that's impossible (you know the old witticism about translations being like women — the more beautiful the less faithful); perhaps so, but doing the impossible sounds like a perfectly ordinary human ambition.

How do you decide that a poem is finished?

There isn't one single way. I read it out loud over and over again. I agonize about whether this bit or that bit is bearable, or whether the whole thing should be quietly forgotten. I make adjustments, and read it again. Then maybe I go back to the earlier reading. I see whether it has takers when I send it out. If it doesn't, I agonize a little more. I leave it around for some time, forget about it, and then look at it again. This is just part of my managing an obsession as if it were a job. I may even make a few last changes on the proofs of the collection it goes in. I may even revise it before re-publishing ...

Who do you write for? Do you have a particular audience or person in mind?

I have a shadowy sense of a small readership. It's got a dark centre of people I know well and a penumbra with no clear limit of people I may know to some extent, or barely at all. It's perhaps even beginning to extend into the light of people who are completely unknown to me, and whose response remains a total mystery. Do I write for them? Well, I write for whoever cares to read what I write. Occasionally poems are also dedicated to particular people, or include events that were shared with friends, or pay homage to other writers. I also write for myself, because the poems have to give me pleasure or I don't see how they could reasonably give anybody else any.

Does poetry have to be 'simple' to get an audience?

No, I don't think so. Nor do I think poetry that provides no obvious problems of surface understanding — like Blake's 'Tiger' — is necessarily simple.

Which contemporary poets do you most admire?

Roy Fisher. There are many others that I can enjoy reading (e.g. Mark Ford, Elaine Feinstein, James Lasdun, Bill Manhire, Jo Shapcott . . .) but I admire Roy Fisher.

What is it about Roy Fisher's work that you find most admirable?

Much of the poetry I read, however different from what I could do myself, conveys thoughts and feelings which I've either had, know about and would prefer not to have, or which it's not too hard to imagine myself having; with Roy Fisher I read the productions of a sensibility that either gives me something that I don't have in my equipment at all, or which unearths things in my experience and sensibility that I wasn't aware of having. Whereas the poetry I enjoy tends to nudge me in stimulating ways I recognize, his poetry positively elbows me out of my habitual thought patterns. Being familiar with his writings doesn't seem to have changed this experience of reading it at all.

That's what I admire about his work; what I admire about him is that he's gone on doing what he does without getting too worked up by what everyone else is doing and saying, has only written when he feels he has to, has not felt the urge to push his work that hard, or promote himself too much. He doesn't attack other poets in print, and thinks that there are a host of ways to make poetry, none of which has got any prior claim to authority or is going to guarantee success in the enterprise. I admire all that, and wish I could better emulate it.

Which trends in modern poetry do you find most interesting?

I don't find trends interesting; they're for the literary journalists to do crowd control exercises. Also, there are so many poetic cultures in the world, and so many different agendas, that if you think you know what the trends are, then you are probably excluding most of them from your picture before you wonder about the question. Cubist? Apocalyptic? Movement? L=A=N=G? Deep Image? Pomo? New-Gen? Who cares? I like individual works by particular poets.

Does poetry have any influence outside poetry?

The puzzle for me in your question comes from the spatial metaphor implied by 'outside'. This could mean either 'outside poems' or 'outside the poetry world'. Apart from the literal sense of the words in the text and the words not in it, I don't understand what 'inside poems' could mean. Also the words in the poem only have sense because they are part of a language that includes all the other words not in the poem: so the words not in the poem are necessary to the words in it, and the words in it need also to be understood as they are used when not in the poem. Then again, the 'poetry world': what is it? Just an intersecting sub-set of the one world we all have to inhabit. So I don't think there's such a place as 'inside' poetry or 'outside' it. As for your version of Auden's 'poetry makes nothing happen' issue, I believe it has no end of influences; but you can't touch them, or quantify them, and people don't like to talk about them.

In his recent book Unweaving the Rainbow, *Richard Dawkins claims that poets have not understood the poetry of science — the title comes from Keats' criticism of scientists. Would you agree that this antagonism still exists? Do we really still live in Snow's two cultures?*

That brother nearest to me in age is a research scientist at the National Physical Laboratory, and we played out the old two cultures argument as a sibling rivalry theme. I haven't read Dawkins' book, so can't comment on that specifically, but it looks from what you say as if he's using the word 'poetry' in the phrase 'the poetry of science' to mean not poems about science, but the poetical as it can be found in scientific research. There are good poems involving science and not so good ones, and then there are poems not about science that simply take the applied facts of scientific experiment and technological development for granted. My brother did some research on the use of electron beam interferometry for the better identification of metal fatigue in, among other things, aeroplanes (more 'jet lag and birdsong').

There are some societal reasons for the antagonism. You could think it was a bit rich for scientists to say that poets don't understand 'the poetry of science', when scientists tend to give poetry such short shrift and assume that it's the poets who have failed to do the understanding. This happens because scientists are, as Wittgenstein noted, the acknowledged high priests and mythmakers of our culture. They are the hierophants at the temple dedicated to 'the meaning of the universe' — and if the poets want to get back a bit of their lost cultural kudos (it seems to be implied) they'd better get their thinking caps on and spend more time in the conceptual lab, less in the imaginary museum.

I have been as awe-struck and flummoxed as the next person about the idea of time going backwards, space being curved, of black holes, event horizons, and big bangs, at the miracles of evolutionary biology which produced the frontal lobes to be awestruck with, or at the square root of minus-one . . . But none of it makes me feel the need to write a poem coming on, and so, for me, that's all there is to it. I'm glad scientists helped develop the technology for the CT scan, mentioned in 'Hearing Difficulties' from *Lost and Found*, and minutely accurate brain surgery (see 'A Burning Head' in the same collection) without which I'd have died a lingering, inexplicable death; I wish they hadn't split the atom and developed the Bomb or the nuclear power station — the Chernobyl accident's fall-out in rain on East Anglia being my private explanation for the brain tumour's triggering . . .

What use do you make of the internet? Do you maintain a website or use e-mail groups to display your work-in-progress?

I use it to try and keep in touch. It has eased the sense of isolation I feel living in Japan. I haven't set up a website yet, but one is in construction and it may be up this year. I don't belong to any e-mail group specifically for workshop-type activity, and the one list I'm on is too hairy and eclectic a place to ask for comments on the fine-tuning of a caesura. But, as I say, e-mail contact means that I can send new poems out to people for comment much more quickly and efficiently than in the past.

What are you working on at the moment?

I've just about finished a new collection of poems, begun in December 1993, which will probably be called *The Colouring of the Past*. There's the manuscript of the *Complete Poems of Vittorio Sereni* that Marcus Perryman and I are hoping to have published soon. I've a number of critical projects and translations manuscripts in progress. Just recently I've returned to some unfinished stories too. There's also a chapbook's worth of very new poems that may be publishable somewhere before too long. I've more, but that's surely enough to be getting along with . . .

TWO

Through frosted glass

IAN SANSOM: *John Ashbery recently described your work as 'curiously strong' and you've also been called the finest poet of your generation. You've published two collections with Carcanet, a book of critical essays with OUP; you've edited the poems of Adrian Stokes and a book of essays on Geoffrey Hill, as well as two poetry magazines,* Perfect Bound *and* Numbers; *you've published numerous essays and reviews, and you won the 1988 Cheltenham Prize, yet your work still seems hardly known here in England. Why?*

Perhaps it's something to do with not being in one or two rumpus-making anthologies, or not doing many readings, or not seeming to represent any salient faction or minority, or writing poems that are like frosted glass: neither polemically opaque nor transparently popular. Perhaps I have some loyal readers but, as you say, I haven't been granted a large audience yet.

What do you think Ashbery meant by 'curiously strong'?

Your guess is as good as mine. Perhaps he had somewhere in the back of his mind a little magazine edited by Ian Patterson that was called *The Curiously Strong*, also named after the mints. He's having fun with Harold Bloom's 'strong' poets who rewrite the metaphors of the world, or whatever, and maybe we 'curiously strong' are more interested in giving the world as it is some oblique attention. Actually, I took it as a funny way of paying a compliment to poems by younger writers such as Mark Ford whose work he happened to like.

In the preface to In the Circumstances *you state your belief in 'poetry as a response to other lives and the otherness of those lives.'*

That phrase was written by one of the anonymous reporters on the text I submitted to OUP. I lifted it because it seemed to sum up an aspect of what I was trying to get at in the various chapters. There's a thread of poetry associated with the familiar style, that is full of other people and their differences: from before Ben Jonson to Frank O'Hara and beyond. Those kinds of poem that take place between people are ones I'm particularly drawn to.

So how would you reply to the reviewer of Entertaining Fates *who described your work as solipsistic?*

Timothy Harris thought he detected in *me*, not my work, what he called 'a self-absorption amounting almost, if not in fact to, solipsism.' The personal note in his review was unfortunate. He doesn't know me. Stephen Romer wrote to the magazine in which that remark appeared expressing his disgust with the review and calling the charge of solipsism 'absurd'. It was a kind gesture from a friend who I like to believe exists independently of my consciousness of his existence. Last year a benign tumour was taken out of my brain in an operation that required a twenty-four hour anaesthetic. Parma, playing at Wembley, had won the European Cup Winner's Cup while I was unconscious. Piazza Garibaldi had been full of other people celebrating the victory, having their feelings whether I lived or died. It was very reassuring. Harris's review came out during my convalescence. Why was he so angry? Many of the poems in that book, and especially the long one called 'Confetti', are expressly about other people's feelings. Harris's depression may relate to the difficulties involved in writing about intimate situations while wishing to preserve some degree of anonymity and privacy. The poems are like frosted glass in this too: they half reveal and half conceal their occasions.

Is that true of the poems in This Other Life *about witnessing the rape of a companion?*

Yes, it is, though there's not much mistaking the occasion there. One or two readers have said they felt uncomfortable reading those poems. Why shouldn't they? A reviewer accused me of re-raping the girl by writing them. The person involved kindly relieved me of guilt on that particular count. What can I say? It happened, and it happened to me too, in that I was forced to witness it at gunpoint. It took place when we were both twenty-two years old, so that practically everything I've written has been shadowed by that far-off event. By enduring what she did, she probably saved both our lives. I felt circumstantially responsible for what happened, and ashamed of my own sex . . . and much more that I can't possibly talk about here. The poems were written between 1979 and 1985 — eight short poems in seven years, between four and ten years after the fact. They were trying to make something good out of an unspeakable blank in both our youths.

You seem fascinated by silences, those moments when language falters or fails.

Yes, silences are places where poetry starts and stops, where taboo subjects wait to be touched on. If there's something that can't be said, poetry might try to make it sayable, or find a way of pointing to what remains to be intuited.

But isn't that just an English obsession with embarrassment and awkwardness?

I'm English; and I can be evasive, it's true. I don't enjoy head-on confrontation, because usually someone is simplifying matters to score a point or inflict pain, but I doubt that this explains it. After all, much French poetry since Mallarmé has been obsessed with silence. Paul Celan's poems are fretted with silence. Silence is the normal circumstance in which poems are sounded.

Would you be prepared to admit that your descriptions of silences are themselves self-protective, elusive?

Maybe so; as I say, my poems are often about what Giles Foden once called 'our most private and troubled moments' and if phrases come to me that touch on such moments they will be pointing towards some hinterlands of human relations that can't simply be put in the poem. Then, however based on particular experiences, poems need to stand relatively alone. If the reader cannot tell who I'm talking to or why, as someone recently complained, then suffice to say that I don't think the reader needs to know. Readers are free to disagree.

Do you think silence can be positive?

In formal gardens here they have a bamboo device that sends a drop of water into a pond at intervals just to emphasize the silence.

And your sensitivity to moments of linguistic awkwardness translates into your deployment of what might be called difficult syntax?

In my first book, *Overdrawn Account*, some of the syntax is over-consciously trying to turn in unpredictable ways. In *This Other Life* there is an attempt to make stanzas of complex sentences that contain and bring forward various meanings simultaneously. In *Entertaining Fates* I allowed syntactic crevices that the reader might, as Browning once advised, leap over. More recently, the sentences have become a little simpler, perhaps. Syntax is always an issue for me because the poems come into my head as snatches of lineated rhythmic phrasing, rarely as complete clauses; and it is not always possible to produce plain prose syntax without introducing filler that ruins everything. I compose the bits hoping they'll resonate, keep their freshness, and convey enough narrative or continuous sense to communicate with readers. Certainly I don't set out to mystify — quite the contrary.

When did you start writing poetry?

I began at the usual moment. Between the ages of fifteen and seventeen, writing poems developed from a kind of prank into an obsession. I couldn't exactly reconstruct all the stages. We were studying the Metaphysical poets and Joyce's *A Portrait* for A-level. There was a dedicated English teacher called Alan Hodgkinson who gave me a copy of *Ulysses* to read. Rebelling against my father (an Anglican minister), getting drunk and going out with girls, I was lent Bob Dylan's LPs by someone slightly older. There was a copy of T. S. Eliot's selection of Pound, and a volume of Robert Lowell in a Liverpool bookshop. Mix it all up and there I am painting pictures, learning to play the guitar, and imitating the *Songs of Innocence and Experience*, aspiring to the latter, betraying the former: a fairly standard case history for a would-be poet born in the coronation year.

Do you feel part of any English tradition?

My mother's relatives were working people from the North East, and I feel affection for Basil Bunting. My father's brother wore himself out in the Birmingham car industry and Roy Fisher was the poet who most helped me find my way when young. I grew up singing George Herbert before becoming aware that he had written what I had in my mouth. More recently, experience has made me feel close to Elizabeth Bishop's poems about loss and travel. Well, I could go on mentioning poets I've felt affinities with for a long time, and the list probably wouldn't add up to any single tradition.

How did your work on Adrian Stokes affect your poetry?

Thanks to Donald Davie, I came to Adrian Stokes through Pound. It was almost immediately after that rape happened. I had just begun graduate studies, and there, as if by chance, help was at hand: Stokes writes about the wholeness of other people being reinforced through art, and about attack and reparation in the making of sculptures, paintings and poems.

You've also translated work by several poets, most notably Vittorio Sereni. What attracted you to him?

I came across Franco Fortini's 'To Vittorio Sereni' in Hamburger's translation, and then noticed a remark Montale made about one of Sereni's books: 'But the difficulty starts when one is forced to live on what is the very opposite of poetry, accepting the risks, the torments and the necessity of camouflaging oneself beneath the *modus vivendi* of the man in the street. Such poetry, which should logically lead to silence is nevertheless obliged to be eloquent.' The man on the street, that silence, and the obligation to be eloquent all sounded interesting. Marcus Perryman did some rough drafts and I started working on them. That was fourteen years ago, when I couldn't speak a word of Italian. Sereni was another Godsend. His work is about how circumstantial guilt can damage the ability to live fully: when faced with the invasion of Sicily, he let himself be captured, missed the civil war of 1943-5, and never quite recovered from his existence as a POW. My father was traveling the length of Italy with the British forces during the two years he spent in Algerian prison camps. Vittorio Sereni was also the kindest poet I ever met. The rape we've been talking about took place on a road somewhere between Milan and the Northern Italian Lakes, where Sereni was born. Working on him helped to transform a nightmarish sense of Italy into something much more benevolent.

Do you feel at home now in Japan?

Not very, but it's a safe and unthreatening place where I can earn a living and am allowed time to write and research. There's an intermittent tradition of having poets as foreign lecturers in my department. It begins with Ralph ('How delightful to meet Mr') Hodgson; then there's George Barker, James Kirkup, and me: a motley crew, but at least writing poems here is assumed to be natural. For a foreigner not to feel at home in Japan is normal. But not feeling at home in England where I didn't find a job, where my marriage went wrong, and where the political culture has been going through a long drawn out phase of moral and managerial self-deception, hypocrisy, and contempt for others . . . that's a different matter, because I love England and have good reasons to be grateful to its Health Service — among the country's greatest achievements, I think.

Your work has always engaged with serious moral questions.

Well, I would say 'ordinary' rather than 'serious.'

Yes, but you take your responsibilities as a poet seriously.

A poet's responsibilities go in more than one direction. There's the work and there are the lives from which it comes and to which it returns. Yeats wrote that 'The intellect of man is forced to choose / Perfection of the life, or of the work.' No choice at all, really. Joyce's story 'A Painful Case', written years before, shows up that false distinction. If you choose perfection of the work, you'll mess up your life, and that will, in turn, mess up your work. If you choose perfection of the life, you're either a saint or deluded. Larkin, I think, took Yeats's 'The Choice' seriously, or used it as an alibi for not marrying Monika or Maeve. Motion's biography and the *Selected Letters* give glimpses of the sorry pickle he produced by trying to live 'a writer's life.' F. T. Prince recently wrote encouraging me not to worry too much as there is no such thing as an immaculate oeuvre, just as there is no such thing as an immaculate life. Perhaps the point is to try and make the life and the work good enough.

Terry Eagleton called your critical essays pretentious, didn't he?

As far as reviews are concerned I've been around long enough to have experienced the good, the bad, and the ugly. Eagleton states that, 'For Robinson, poems are open to what he somewhat pretentiously calls their "otherness".' The word 'otherness' is adopted from the critical writings of Stokes, and he developed it from the psychoanalytic theories of Melanie Klein. It has also been elaborated by the philosopher Richard Wollheim in relation to both those authors. My only innovation is to apply the ideas to ways of making and reading poems, something that Stokes had begun to do. If I'm being pretentious by doing this, at least I can console myself with the thought that I'm in good company.

Both in your poems and in In the Circumstances *you seem torn between the idea that poetry has a duty to make amends and the belief that such an ambition is misplaced. How do you explain the apparent contradiction?*

26

An early poem of mine is called 'Some Hope'. We need hope in facing what life throws at us, and in trying to repair damage to our shop-soiled world; yet how could I imagine that trying to make amends by producing poems can make a difference? I'd like poems to be disarming . . . but then I would have to be 'curiously strong' not to need defences.

In Leaf-viewing *there seems to be a change of tone. The poem 'Leaving Sapporo', about a missed plane, begins, 'This had not happened before'; there seems a certain relief in that, and the poem ends, 'blame the unforeseen through which we live . . . but, yourself, forgive.' An earlier poem, 'In Summer Wind' ends, 'you know it isn't in me / to judge, forgive myself, still less forget.' Are you learning to forgive yourself?*

Landing in Japan, I found a place in which many of the concerns that had haunted me in England, and which get expressed in *Entertaining Fates*, were not relevant. One recent poem represents the words of a Japanese colleague saying: 'Put away the personal sensations.' It isn't possible, but I was grateful for the opportunities working here offered. 'In Summer Wind' ends by adapting the conclusion from Sereni's poem 'First Fear': 'On my own / I cannot bring myself to justice.' It's not for me to forgive myself and I have a painfully good memory for some things; but I can ask Teruhiko Nagao, the dedicatee of the Sapporo poem, to forgive himself, because this is something difficult for Japanese people to do, I understand, and they go to lengths to avoid loss of face for this reason. As regards making amends, you might think that the poem does this; but then it also inscribes Professor Nagao's embarrassment into tablets of stone. You could think it made matters worse. I'm glad to report that the person concerned didn't feel that way. In the year that produced 'In Summer Wind', I started on a novel about the circumstantial responsibility that we talked about earlier. Its narrator observes at one point that feeling guilty can be a form of self-importance. It's my belief that you can't forgive yourself; you have to be forgiven. However, you can try to give up taking on so much blame for unforeseen mishaps and calamities. Perhaps that's what I've done.

THREE

The torque in poetic talk

MARCUS PERRYMAN: *So why do you write poetry?*

There are innumerable possible impulses for writing poems, but my basic answer to your question would have to be that I'm habituated to writing poetry as a way of knowing myself. That 'knowing myself' could be understood in many ways of course, but it would include being able to tell what counts and what doesn't. I have drafts, poems, or half-poems whose value to me, and to no one else, is that they showed where I was attempting to make myself feel something I didn't, or following a sensation that proved trivial, sentimental, or just dead. The poem might have not come off or have gone wrong for a technical reason, but I tend to think that technical problems have implications to take personally.

The Socratic recommendation about knowing yourself begs a lot of questions, though: and Wittgenstein would wonder just what is the language game of knowing yourself, as opposed to knowing the date, or knowing how to play chess, or other types of knowing. So what kind of knowing is it, and why is this achieved, in your case, in writing poetry rather than prose?

Part of knowing yourself would involve a Wittgensteinian knowing what the verb could mean when it takes that reflexive object. Given the theoretical importance placed on language in recent years, it might be tempting to say that 'I know English' and 'I know myself' were practically synonymous. That we don't use them as synonyms starts a lot of hares. Still, knowing the language well would likely count as contributing much to whatever self-knowledge were understood to be. So then writing prose could count, for others, and sometimes me, as a means of self-knowledge too.

The difference, as far as I'm concerned, lies in the distinction that some have noted between composing and writing. Poetry, as I understand it, cannot be just written. It has to form itself as rhythmical units, preferably in the head, sometimes on paper. These rhythmical units, phrases or sentences, with or without an enjambed turn or two, are intolerant of 'filler': they can't be mashed into whatever grammatical shape I happen to fancy. Nor do they incline themselves to fit into a predetermined stanza-form. Finding the shape and the grammar involves discovering what the phrases mean to say, where they need to go, what they're telling me.

'What the phrases mean to say' puts the poet in the position of listening, rather than writing, and filtering the words that come to mind into a poem. Has it always been that way for you, or did you set out with more deliberation? Was Overdrawn Account *a conscious choice of subject matter related to place, circumstances, things that occurred? There it feels as if the poetry is setting out both to take on circumstances and to resist them. The artistic and human sense of words like 'overdrawn' and 'benefit' are set against their starker banking and bureaucratic meanings.*

When I started to try and write poems in mid-teenage I didn't have the first idea of what is was supposed to be like, and no one to ask, except I assumed from school reading that the words were supposed to be not the same as talk. My earliest conscious models were, in fact, Virginia Woolf and James Joyce, with Blake following close on their heels. I just worked up a froth of language that both carried and concealed what was bullying me.

Overdrawn Account is part project and part ragbag of early things. It's not well put together as a collection. 'The Benefit Forms', my first pamphlet publication, is a sequence attempting to give some shape to what were to be my last experiences of living in the North of England. But it was in the process of writing and then revising and re-revising those early poems that I started to get a sense of what sounded right and what seemed like fustian. The joins between the bits in those early pieces are sometimes rather rough-cut, partly because I couldn't connect them and partly because the poetic climate was telling me that disjunctions were preferred.

'Overdrawn Account', the title piece, written in September 1976, was one of the first poems that 'came to me': I just jotted down the first seven lines, as published, one night before going to bed, and then got up the next morning and put together, rather more consciously it has to be said, the following twenty-one. That experience of having poems that came out quickly or smoothly and, thus, surprised me, was a pointer towards this process of listening for things, learning to recognize words making themselves felt, and developing means for responding to them. So, yes, in the early work I'm taking on the circumstances, which does also imply that I'm struggling with them. That's probably what I've always done, but there was less listening and more striving at the outset.

Making ends meet, and making amends meet and fitting, seem to be the background subject matter of Overdrawn Account *and* This Other Life. *Have things been repaired or has reparation just been impossible? Maybe this sounds like I'm talking about your life not your poetry, but you don't seem to be a poet who likes to distinguish between them. The otherness of the other life is both others and writing, I take it.*

You take it right, and your puns point to what couldn't be combined. It proved impossible both to make ends meet and to make amends meet. If manageable at all, making amends, I discovered, absolutely requires a continuing shared life in which the reparative actions can register. Reparations to the dead must actually be to surviving relatives, comrades, or whatever. Making ends meet involved moving to Japan, where I was able to mitigate the overworked and underpaid slide of my English years. Emigration was also one of the final nails in the coffin of my first marriage. The problems and paradoxes with these interrelations between art and life have led me to back off, a little, more recently. Now I try to get the poems to sound right and let the implications of that 'rightness' look after themselves as best they can.

How do you measure a poem's 'sounding right'? What do the sounds, rhythms, and sense of the words correspond to? And how do you make it correspond to what the reader should be noticing, i.e. how do you make it both sound right and give over its contents?

Let's go back to the idea of poetry being composed by listening: are the words hearing themselves? Does the spoken sound contour of the words and phrases, as it moves and swerves forward, echo and twist back? There has to be torque in poetic talk. This is one way that a poem can hear itself think. You might call it the aesthetic version of the coherence theory of truth, the difference being that the truth is generated by the formed concords and discords in the composed language, as sound and statement, rather than the requirements of philosophical logic.

Then the words have to echo and twist back in another sense: as in Johnson's remarking of Gray's Elegy that 'the bosom returns an echo'. That the words sound together, producing a concerted effect, has also to be caught in flight by the equipment of a person hearing.

The poet must be the text's 'test flight' reader. So: does the poem correspond with the poet's mind and body? What correspondences with the world are registered in that correspondence? You can see here that I'm implying an aesthetic version of the correspondence theory of truth, one in which 'fit' is judged by auditory and conceptual hit or miss, rather than by analytical criteria. If the answers coming back are positive, then it's time to start finding out if the poem will correspond with anybody else's bosom. The wish, hope, gamble is that if it works for me then it stands a chance of working for you. But that's always going to be a risk.

You ask about 'what the reader should be noticing'. This could be taken in either predictive or obligational senses. 'Readers should notice that there's a first-person speaker addressing an unnamed second-person interlocutor' could mean that I expect readers will notice this if they look at the poem in even a quite cursory fashion, or that they must or ought to notice it — or they won't have read the thing properly. Now, while it's possible to conduct school or university exams on the basis of the second type of 'should', it's only possible for me to write poems and have relations with readers on the basis of the first.

This is why I don't tend to use 'in your face' difficulty if I can avoid it, and like to have a situation or story that I'm addressing, even if quite obliquely, so that what the reader can be expected to notice is the setting, the scenery, the participants, the basic situation. What the poem is then communicating by means of these things is going to be a shade more indeterminate, I expect, because in order to be true to even quite restricted human situations and responses to them it's going to have to be many-faceted, and the way to do that in art is, I think, to recess the complexity into the poetic structure, which can then be caught by reading and looking again at the composed words. What I meant by letting the implications look after themselves amounts to this: if the poem is a good one, then the more the reader can hear in it, the more it will be conveying. There are experienced readers and less experienced ones. I can't not but write for experienced ones; yet even such readers may, of course, be resistant to certain forms of echo chamber. Still, I can't legislate about how much a reader should be able to hear.

I mention the 'get over to the reader' aspect only because I think you have been considered at times 'obscure' and at others 'too close to the bone'. A

31

situation may be less in the foreground now or far further back, as if its complexity ousts the situation itself. It is as if you were saying 'Don't get distracted by the context.' Is this a reaction to people finding the poems about witnessing a rape in This Other Life *unsettling? Is it the basic difference between that book and* Lost and Found *(Entertaining Fates seeming to fall somewhere between)? I mean, you seem to have rarefied the contexts, or it has become less important to flesh them out.*

If you write about things others have not experienced, or can't have experienced in quite the same way, then there may well be an unavoidably unsettling sense to get over. But let's get the 'obscurity' and 'near the bone' issues into perspective. There is plenty of poetry around that makes mine look as clear as crystal and plain as day. I get called those things, very occasionally, because my writings tend to be situated in a fairly reader-friendly style, but then the going may get tricky. Still, there have been changes. It used to be that I had burdensome experiences that I needed to externalize and bring into some focus. These were partly accidents of biography. The experience of publishing over many years has also played a part. Looking back at poems of mine that I can read with pleasure, I couldn't help noticing that the autobiographical urgency or personal subject had usually evaporated with time, but the poem didn't seem to have. So the autobiographicality was a means to an end: it might have been that what mattered was that this was *my* life or *me* saying it, but time had made this a life among others and someone happening to say it. Writing now I may be better at concentrating on the aspects of the occasion that will foreground the ends, and back-pedaling the autobiographical means; or I may be able to deploy the autobiographical without being so ensnared in it. But, as I say, this is the area of risk: there are many kinds of reader out there, and many kinds of poem. You can't please everyone all the time, and that may well not quite be the point of the exercise anyway.

John Ashbery has described you as like a peppermint: 'curiously strong'. What do you think he meant?

There's a likelihood that Ashbery's remark is being over-interpreted if it is taken to mean anything more than a witty slogan. If I were to read it in a way that suits me, then it would seem to be saying that these poets (I was part of a list) are curious about the world in a strong way, and that this produces poems in which curiosity is strongly rewarded. This is to understand the remark as a rebuke to the ways Richard Rorty has adapted Harold Bloom's idea as praise for the poet at the expense of the analytic philosopher. He tries to do away with the need to take seriously either the coherence or the correspondence theory of truth, and of any responsibility to accurate representation — or so it seems. Being 'strong' means not bothering about that supposedly defunct aesthetic morality; so perhaps the 'curiously strong' are not so sanguine about that grand theory, and ready to credit the world with an autonomous existence that deserves respectful curiosity.

Rather astoundingly you've also been accused of solipsism. Apart from the above, which would itself be a defence against such an accusation, what would you say? Or rather, how do you think such an idea might arise?

I've responded to this twice already, once in a letter to *PN Review*, and again in an interview with Ian Sansom. In both cases I defended myself against the charge. Time having passed, and the world changed without my say-so, that seems unimportant now. Timothy Harris's phrase 'a self-absorption amounting almost, if not in fact to, solipsism' might be aiming at, but failing to hit through the *ad hominem*, a complexity of lyric poetry, and perhaps of art more generally. The equipment that can make you curious and responsive to the world is only going to be registering sensitively if you are attending closely to it. It's not difficult to see, for example, Wordsworth as a poet who is vastly self-absorbed and therefore acutely responsive to the effect on him of external stimuli. No doubt this responsiveness through attentiveness to sensations and language, being so delicate a balance, can be upset. Harris may have felt that there were poems in *Entertaining Fates* where the balance had shifted from the external world because it was stuck on the attunement of the equipment, but he was wrong to accuse me, rather than the poems he was reading, of a moral-aesthetic failure. This was partly the burden of that letter, the only one I've yet written responding to a review.

If the topic is inter-personal damage, the subject can be registered by noting in the poems that the vividness of the world is fogged by the damage, as in 'my ill-founded fear / spoiling fresh, perpetual / movement through firm grass / wind gusts part and comb . . .' — 'Easter Break' in the collection Harris reviewed, or 'a garden's plum and bamboo tree / skeined in sadness, love, / and you can't lift the veil' — 'As We Found It' in *Lost and Found*. A reviewer inclined to find fault might pick on these observations and say that the speaker is just wrapped up in himself, but that would be to misread, I believe, and to miss a number of points about poems: for instance, in order to describe what you feel you've lost you have to make it fairly vivid (as I hope I do in the lines above), and in consequence the figure who is experiencing the events in a lyric poem can only be partially identified with the person who has written it. After all, among many differences, the former is usually innocent of the fact that he or she is taking part in a poem — a point that helps to limit the possible infinite regress of literary reflexivity.

Solipsism is one of those philosophical theories that can't be disproved, in that there is no way to have experiences without being the person who's having them, but this being so, as, differently, Berkeley's theory required, the solipsistic character of experience has practically to drop out of the equation — it being unnecessarily pedantic (and a misunderstanding of the social nature of language) to have to add an 'as I see it' after absolutely everything you ever say.

Well, I'd always taken solipsism to mean not self-absorption, but the inability to find any otherness in the world. And Berkeley used to insist that he had simply a common sense view of the world, by saying that it needs to be perceived. So when Johnson strikes his foot on the ground he's actually exemplifying rather than refuting Berkeley's theory. Your version of lyric poetry seems to have a great deal of accommodation for other people's perceptions in it, though, doesn't it?

Perhaps Harris thought like you too, but believed that a bad case of the former would, more or less, equate with the latter (something that doesn't strictly follow, as you suggest). I tend to take solipsism in the Berkeleian sense, because 'the inability to find any otherness in the world' strikes me as more an acute psychological disturbance than a philosophy.

That early reading in Joyce's fiction set me on the road to wondering about the presentation of other consciousnesses in a text, and I'm well aware of the many dangers in an 'I am! yet what I am who cares, or knows?' approach to lyric poetry. This is what drew me to the encounter poems of Wordsworth, to Browning's dramatic lyrics, and to dialogue in Dante and contemporary poetry. I thought it helpful to try whenever possible to locate the lyrical subject in social space, and to populate the space so that this subjectivity showed for what it is: the words of one among many. Articulating conflictual views within the lyric structures, and shading in other implications too, was the best I could do to get the poetic text to shadow more nearly the circumstances and constraints of speaking in specific contexts, while making as full a use as I could of the multiple perspectives to be derived from the fact that this was a poem and not a slice of life.

One justification for such an approach shows in my quarrel with a remark of Yeats's. He wrote memorably but partially that 'We make out of the quarrel with others, rhetoric, but of the quarrel with ourselves, poetry.' The problem with this saying, as Yeats's later poetry makes abundantly clear, is that the quarrel with others doesn't make sense if it isn't also a quarrel we feel within ourselves, and the quarrel with ourselves needs to have its equivalent quarrels with others for it to make sense even to us. Unlike Yeats, though, I have had the benefit of reading philosophers' writings on the private language argument — which brings us round to Wittgenstein once more.

And back to solipsism, too, since the private language argument is effectively about the need for a community to create language and an attack on 'private' sensation. But you've left a trail of things that could be followed. Let me go at Wittgenstein in a different way. Has he been taken up to promote the 'they're all only stories' version of literature? Is he one of the unwitting fathers of the post-modern?

Yes, I think he has, by some. Rorty, for example, will happily round him up with J. L. Austin as a forerunner of his brand of neo-pragmatism with its 'philosophy is all only stories'. But there are others who would take such a strategy as merely a way of shunting Wittgenstein into the history of philosophy, and so not taking him as identifying issues and problems which don't actually get wished away by some smart-ish metaphorical moves.

I'm inclined to hope that the so-called 'post-modern' has just about run its course. The name itself points to it as a 'late' style, a Mannerism in the art historical sense. As such, it's also a highly self-conscious bit of periodization characterized by an identity crisis about whether it's a new period or just the appendix to an old one. There must be chances that in time it will either seem like the 'decadence' at the end of the 19th, or like the early moves in a new cultural formation, like the last decade of the 18th century, or perhaps something entirely its own.

Just as I'm not inclined to think that Rorty has definitively solved the problems of philosophy, so I'm unimpressed by the 'only stories' view of literature. Doesn't it have this in common with Berkeleian solipsism in that it's both common sense, and it cancels out of the equation? The human institutions of speaking and writing are not grounded in a single guaranteed fact-based practice, only in the institutions of narratives; however, if everything is then narrative, there can be, and indeed are, different types of institution.

'In the Twilight', from *Lost and Found*, was set going by hearing someone use the phrase 'the twilight of the real', as if it were another of Nietzsche's gods on the way out. The last line 'a beak darts at its prey' was attempting to ground as much as is necessary the sense that the real cannot be an 'idea' that has passed its sell-by date, in that it is assumed by the creature intent on feeding itself. The heron's real is confirmed by its fishing trip. It's a poetic metaphor for the necessity of linguistic reference — by which I mean that correspondence between words and world is necessarily assumed in all human activities, even sceptical accounts of the posited relationship.

Living in Japan must make the correspondence between words and world a little problematic. 'Leaf-viewing' seems rather caught by the dilemma of only being able to watch things. And 'Nostalgia for the Present' in Lost and Found *seems addressed to the problem of the present — the here and now — and the untense, the tenseless, present: 'nothing more alarming than a topless torso'. The echoes of Vittorio Sereni in the last part of* Lost and Found *are all from* Stella Variabile, *his final and most metaphysical book.*

But the most highlighted allusion to Sereni in that part of the book is the title of the sequence 'A Burning Head', which is lifted out of 'Ancora sulla strada di Zenna' from *Gli strumenti umani* — 'carry round a burning head of sorrow'. That's about returning to his hometown and finding things painfully similar and different. It seemed such a gift for my sequence, which is about undergoing brain surgery, but, more importantly, about returning to England to face up to many changes of affairs both public and private.

'Nostalgia for the Present' has a Sereni-inflected title too, but the idea is from his prose. That poem is presided over by Giorgio de Chirico, because the electric power station at Riva del Garda and some of the lakeside architecture has an early-modern-Italy feel caught in some of his canvasses from after the First War. There are other echoes of his earlier Metaphysical paintings, and he does have a statue somewhere called 'Melancholy', I think. The 'topless torso' is a joke: a girl sunbathing who has taken off her bikini top, or the headless sculpted torso in 'The Uncertainty of the Poet', the combination of the two producing something that could be alarming or not. This is all used to shadow in a sense of the 'tenseless present', one where connections with the past are thinned and the future is mighty uncertain. But it also has the idea of a strongly experienced present, something you could feel nostalgic about wanting to relive even as you're living it. There's equal attraction and disorientation. I'm just deploying bits of 'everyday life surrealism' to catch both.

As for living in Japan, it's true. The whole country is covered with signs in four different scripts (Chinese characters, two Japanese syllabic systems, and the alphabet) and two sets of numerals (Arabic and Japanese). *That* took some getting used to, and though I'm used to it, I'm by no means fully literate. So, yes, the poetic idea of having to scrutinize intensely the world to uncover meaning becomes an everyday problem, and the foreign poet is at least initially an on-looker. But being about Tiananmen Square and the fall of the Eastern European régimes, which all happened in the year I came to Japan, 'Leaf-viewing' (I would suggest) only too accurately catches the feeling of watching while the world changed.

Since beginning to live out of England, I've become much more familiar with the ways different languages fit the part of the world where they are spoken. I appreciate that the relationship is a conventional one, and don't see how it could be any other, but also that this conventional relationship is lived as a vast set of interlocking human institutions. To the people involved in a language use, the word-world relationship seems not merely, but profoundly conventional. Poetry is unimaginable without this enormous 'background' of understandings and competences.

Lost and Found has both a railway station and religious title. The 'memory, loved one, or poem', from 'Lost Objects', seem part and parcel of the same baggage, and when at the end you find yourself, you're wordless and perplexed. Am I wrong, or is there a temptation towards silence in this?

In 'Lost Objects', the speaker is unable to speak for the simple reason that he doesn't know the language. The non-speaker registers a set of losses by not even being able to say for sure what's lost — not least because at the time the poem was written it wasn't altogether clear anyway. So the poem now amounts to a foreboding. This close doesn't seem to me tempted towards silence, not least because it could be said, at the very least, to use reticence as a way of implying volumes. So I don't see myself as one of the many poets in love with the purity of silence, though aware enough of how impure noise can be. Much of the force of poetry comes, after all, from the carefully framed relation between what is spoken out and what is implied, the said and the not said.

Well, you've ducked the issue of religion, and you're not coming too clean on the shift towards metaphysics. But your last but one answer reminded me of another Wittgenstein remark, where he talks about meanings as the things that 'mesh' with our lives. What does your poetry mesh with? Is the religion hovering in it just your family background, or something else?

Something else? I am reluctant to rabbit on about religion and metaphysics, about which I tend to accept that we cannot speak ... But I can talk about how these things as forms of life mesh with poems I've written. The influences of my vicarage childhood are everywhere to be seen, in poems like 'Plain Money', 'In my Father's House', and 'Faith in the City' from *This Other Life*, or parts of 'Confetti' in *Entertaining Fates*. My relationship with it is perhaps summed up by the line 'Restive in the faith that has sustained you', from '472 Claremont Road'.

My father 'takes a good funeral', as they say in the trade, and growing up as I did gave me an early grounding in baptisms, marriages, and burials: the three times that people who aren't religious might find themselves personally involved with a church. So you get introduced into one of the main ways that the culture has institutionalized the 'brass tacks' of birth, copulation and death. That, plus the hymn singing, the psalm chanting, the public prayers and responses, is an introduction to forms of language that have been composed and regularly used to make sense of people's lives ('I once was lost, but now I'm found, / Was blind but now I see.') If you don't happen to believe in the literal existence of a god, or an afterlife, then Christianity is a form of life with a complex morality and a lot of poetry and art attached to it. But I don't think of poetry as a substitute religion; for me, at least, it has been an alternative to religion. It's a means for staying in touch with a view of life that keeps the hard essentials in view, without the need to cotton-wool them in a mythology about sacrifice, sin, and the afterlife that gives me all sorts of problems, far more than it solves. Yet I would still count myself as trying my best to follow Jesus's taxing ethical teachings — his way out of the Old Testament revenge code, for example.

As for metaphysics, my only conscious use for it is in the imagining of how the presence of things absent makes itself felt, and this has more than a little to do with finding meaning in the world. After all, writing itself is a touch metaphysical, being a trace of presence that marks the passing, and therefore absence, of the writer. This territory is one for me to enter in a poem when the need arises, in relation to deaths, or other losses, and the traces that remain, but not something that I have any strong beliefs about. In fact, if I did, then they probably wouldn't need to make themselves felt in poems.

What does my poetry mesh with? The only response I can think of to that is, being made of language composed by a person, it doesn't set out to mesh with anything, and doesn't need to, because its meshing is to be found in, and is assumed by, its language use.

Can you say your poetry has a direction, and if so where is it going now?

The poetry I write seems to me a by-product of my life, and I like to think that so long as my life has a direction, so will the poetry. It's not very likely that people can tell what exactly the direction of their lives is, or if they think they can, mistakes are highly likely. So my poetry's direction might come round to my answer to your opening question: the direction of the poetry is found in discovering what the direction of the life might be.

There's another sense in which the direction of the poetry, like the life, is quite substantially set by the time middle age is reached. I have made many stylistic decisions about what ways of writing poems seem to work for me, and many of them were made at the end of the 1970s, when I'd been writing and publishing for about five years. The aim of these early decisions was to get individual poems to work, but those working choices doubtless included an idea of what might be helpful for the longer run. The sum of these activities amounted to the formation of what I hope has been a flexible style with room in it for surprises, changes of emphasis, and development over the phases of a life. There may well be some surprises in store for me, and for anyone inclined to follow what happens.

As for what the direction of the poetry is, I can't rightly say. The poems I'm able to write will tell me. We'll just have to wait and see.

FOUR

Occasion to revise or think again

MARCUS PERRYMAN: *With some poets you feel there is a hard core of experience around which the poems are gathered or from which they proceed. I'm thinking of Vittorio Sereni, the poet we have translated together, and his poems of wartime and POW experience. Your 'rape' poems, which were first collected as an eight-poem sequence in* This Other Life, *look like the kind of subject matter that might make survival as a human being difficult, let alone as a poet. And critics have thought of this, for instance, as your 'harsh matter'. But aren't there signs of the difficulty of negotiating an intractable reality in earlier poems, or poems you may have written before that experience? I mention Sereni also because I assume that you have a great deal of sympathy with his feeling of being ousted from an event, and failing to take part, repair or make amends for it?*

The events that produced those poems years later took place in September 1975. My girlfriend and I were hitch hiking north from Rome after having almost all our money and most of our documents stolen in the capital. We had made it all the way from the outskirts of the city to somewhere north of Milan in the direction of Como, when we ran out of luck, were picked up by someone with a gun who demanded a sort of in-kind sexual payment (as I imagine he might have seen it) for the lift. So, to avoid being killed, she underwent that 'unutterable humbling' while I waited in the back of the car with a gun pointing at my head. We exchanged a few words in English, to the effect that he might kill us anyway, and what would we do? He didn't understand them, but quickly shut us up; and then when it was over, very surprisingly, he let us go.

We memorized the number-plate of his car as he drove away. All of this took place in the middle of an electric storm. We were both 22 years old. I had written a few poems that would find their way into the first pages of a collected poems, were I to assemble one: 'How He Changes', 'Worlds Apart', and unrevised fragments of 'The Benefit Forms', to be precise. I'd been writing things fairly compulsively for 6 years by then, and, though I can't exactly recover the state of mind, must have seen myself as attempting to find my way following a line of non-metropolitan, northern and north-midlands poets that would include Basil Bunting, Roy Fisher, Charles Tomlinson, and Donald Davie. 'Worlds Apart' is modeled on a Tomlinson poem about an allotment holder. What those poets have in common is some relation to the Poundian line of Modernism, a commitment to the world as recalcitrant and 'other' than the perceiver. So you could say that I had already signed up for a belief in 'negotiating with an intractable reality' before I found myself on the receiving end of something a good deal more intractable than a bit of urban or rural topography.

This 'harsh matter' could not be written about at first, and indeed it took some years before we would even mention it to each other. We went back to Milan for the trial of the man, but never stayed to find out whether he was found guilty. Looking back, it seems like an ordeal that we put ourselves through with gritted teeth. Neither of us received any post-traumatic therapy, or anything like that. She had a fact of violation to experience, brace against, resist, cope with, and move on from; I had something more like the Sereni sense of an event that wrecked our youth, but which didn't even happen to me, and which I was to pass over in silence and to treat as a non-event.

Poems that I wrote in 1977-1978 already have the event in their hinterland (and, naturally enough, my entire work is overshadowed by it): 'Pressure Cooker Noise' has an unusually violent strand inflecting a quotidian kitchen poem; 'Dirty Language' is a dramatic lyric in which the speaker attacks a literary person for domestic passivity; 'Autobiography' is a self-critical farewell to a friend from university with whom I had been having a brief, two-timing relationship just a couple of weeks before the almost fatal sequence of Italian events took place.

How did this sequence take shape and when, as a sequence? Part 1 of This Other Life *is brought together by the family theme, but it is not a sequence. Were you being influenced by the narrative element, the need to tell a story?*

Most of the family poems in Part 1 were written after those in Part 2. I didn't think a reader would be able to stand going right into the book with those rape poems, so put the family material in first, since it forms a continuity from *Overdrawn Account* (1980) — and, in fact, 'A Short History' began with a short passage that wouldn't fit into 'In the Background', wouldn't fit in because it was too much a narrative detail, the bit about my dad preaching from the back of a lorry.

The trajectory of the cycle is into the subject matter, from the return to Italy, to the trial, to the event itself . . . and the emotional focus is sharpest and most poignant in 'Cleaning'. 'Vacant Possession' (with all that those words echo) and 'For Lavinia', as it were, come out of the event again and look at the horror with a no more comfortable or comforted sense. Was this the way you arranged the poems or was it the actual order of composition (and therefore emotional entanglement)?

Those poems were always conceived as an intimately linked group, but I simply didn't have the equipment when I started them to think of writing a narrative about it, and don't think it would have worked either. A narrative poem suggests a degree of ease and fluency regarding the tale to be told that was simply not there. Short lyrics that glance back and then stop were the best I could do. I hoped to sketch the events in these glimpses. The poems were not written in the order they appear. 'From a Memory' was the first, and then 'A September Night' (fragments of it come from a rejected attempt of 1978); it was published twice in magazines with the painfully punning title 'The Counterpane'. That was 1979-80. Then I managed to get a two-verse version of 'There Again', and 'Cleaning' in 1980. Then I did 'The Harm' and 'Vacant Possession' in 1981. I can remember working on 'A Trial' in 1980-81, but only added it to the sequence late in the day. As I say, 'For Lavinia' is an epilogue from 1985. There were a number of others that didn't seem satisfactory. It did also seem clear that the sequence had to be short — as 'For Lavinia' underlines. I went back through the entire experience of 1975 over a few years a decade after when writing the unpublished fictionalized version that I think of as being called *September in the Rain*.

The first poem is called 'There Again', a title whose significance flickers: it is a return but also an occasion for second thoughts. Yet even the second thoughts flicker. I take the line 'like mitigating circumstances' to mean both the normal sense of the expression (in the second thoughts vein) but also the mitigation of circumstances i.e. part of the negotiation of the intractable. The 'unutterable humbling' has a memory of Tennyson's 'innumerable bees', and I take the humbling to mean humiliation . . .

No, it means 'humbling'; maybe humiliation is included in the area of implication, but I don't think she was humiliated by deciding to undergo that experience rather than commit us to a more dangerous response. She rose to it. However, it was also obviously ghastly and damaging, not least to the pride of youth — hers and mine. And here's where the complexity of writing poems impinges. It has been said that 'humbling' is the wrong word because it's truer of what it felt like for me, then for her. Yet I think it's the right word, and not because it 'describes' either my experiences or hers (mine were something like shock, fear, incredulous relief, anger, and then silence and denial). To change the word to 'humiliation' — too abstract, too knowing, too obvious — would wreck the poem; 'humbling' is something being done to her, and to me (I'm speaking and writing it). It doesn't describe, it re-experiences it in its own terms, terms that try to draw upon the balms of sound and delicacy.

But the words of the poem are attuned to echo with words close to them: the word 'relieve' sinisterly ghosts over the fatal word 'relive'. Even the word 'driven' resonates and flickers, with a shade of sex drive, and 'driven mad'. 'Object' with its grammatical undertone and 'serve' turn on similar flickers. And when finally we reach the 'occasion to revise or think again' it positively shrieks with a sense of damage and the need to do something about it. The poem concludes with a different view (echoed in another poem) that seems to invoke a very literal form of negotiation, i.e. a long conversation in words and deeds to reach a common experience, a common ground, and an end to a certain kind of living, to youth, say, and the beginning of a form of difficult co-existence with others, one's own past, and a new, and harsher, form of 'otherness'. It looks, in other words, like a negotiation between familiarity, intimacy and estrangement.

I'm grateful to the meanings of words for the possibilities that are opened up by their ordinary uses. They are what help generate these constructions of a counter-weight to the burden of experience.

I don't think definitions of art get very far, but art has something necessarily to do with survival. It's a way of overcoming something, and living on. Did this cycle have this purpose?

I was young and had the idea that poetry ought to be able to heal me, to heal my love, and benefit life. I had to write those poems, because their burden was making itself felt both in my life and in the other poems I was writing. It seemed to me that I was producing poems no one would ever understand because the crucial thing they were 'about' was not being said. So those eight poems were written to free other poems from side effects, and make it possible to write about other things too. The extent to which I succeeded in any of this is inevitably in question — but I certainly made it impossible for anyone reading my work with any sustained attention to be unaware of this fact about it.

The original second poem in the rape cycle, 'A Trial' is in two different forms, a long preamble, with a tricky grammatical structure, then 3 verses which are not quite quatrains, where the thought looks a little grafted on. So, formally, the poem seems unsuccessful, and I'd like to look into the reasons for this. The subject matter and tone equally split over the hiatus at the centre of the poem. It begins with the same flickering feel of 'There Again': where suspected innocence tilts the word 'innocence' towards a guilty culpability (a trespass against the 'common sense' floated at us in the first poem of the sequence — only there with a vengeance) i.e. she was ingenuous. And then you are asked to acquit yourself of the charge of pimping by denying payment. Here the situation is enough to jar and stir. Then the young interpreter is introduced and looks, herself (the feel is of the interpreter being a woman) a victim, caught up in this 'process' . . .

'A Trial' has got more characters in it than the rest of the sequence put together. Since publishing it in *This Other Life* I've made some small revisions to a few of them, but no sooner had I published 'A Trial' than I began to have doubts about it. I've tried to revise it; but I can't. It's had to be dropped. There, the obligation to give some of the story has defeated the lyrical impulse. It reads to me like a note for the trial chapter of *September in the Rain* — which I wrote about five years later.

Let's come to 'From a Memory'. The title makes precisely what memory is — in this context — rather difficult to understand. The grammar is fostering a sense of 'Memoir' i.e. something deliberately composed (generally for self-glorification) but at the same time it's claiming to be partial and flawed. It's from a memory, but it isn't the memory. The effect is of images being snatched at, 'disordered' as the opening line says, with its reference to the trees used in Italy to line cemeteries. The opening stanza may carry a hint of the ruffled trees in Sereni's great poem 'On the Zenna Road Again'. Your poem ends with 'that pink blank of a wall' which registers a series of conflicts: the finger-pointing of 'that' (where an accusation is escaping onto an object), the skin-coloured blankness like an illegible face, and the wall, a barrier you can't manoeuvre around or negotiate yourself across. The poem is framed against the necessary indifference of the world: the

bedraggled strands flurrying, the dolls in plastic bags (fear of the need for
an abortion?), the irritating flies, tatty, squalid othernesses getting on with
their own existences, as if the one thing that makes these things meaningful
(a human sense) has been sucked out of them. This seems to be the thing
remembered rather than the objects themselves. At the end of your poem
memory makes the present become blurred (not the past), a mere contre-jour,
a counterfeit, and there are no details in life to feed off, just a blankness,
that Shakespearian word you're so fond of. And this is precisely the Serenian
feeling of being ousted from life. Some of these Sereni echoes may have been
deliberate, but others I suspect were not. Is that so?

The idea of trying to render an inert thing responsive — as in 'The
Yellow Tank' from *Lost and Found* (1997), for instance — seems to have
got under my skin. But I think it was there in experiences of decaying
urban environments before September 1975, and Adrian Stokes writes
about the aesthetic experience of cities in more or less those terms:
contemporary art as a compensatory response to an environment
without resonance and echo. But I note that 'the sky, like a blank
drawing board' in 'How He Changes' — from that late spring or
early summer of 1975 — is a blankness of potential and possibility:
that's a distant glimpse of my perhaps culpably innocent, youthful
optimism.

What you say describes just why I feel so close to Sereni's poetry.
His must be the most important in my life, and I read something of
his work almost every day. But when I started on those poems, and
when I drafted 'From a Memory' in 1979, I had not read a word of
it. All those echoes are entirely fortuitous. I don't think the dolls in
plastic bags were prompted by the fear of an abortion. That possibility
had been quickly ruled out in 1975. It was just the sense of a contrast
between these inert objects that are treated fondly and used as things
to remember with, and an animate person being treated like a thing.
The idea for the revised title was that it was taken from *my* memory
— except for the one detail about the tie that is plainly from hers, via
mine. As for 'that pink blank of a wall', I've never been quite able to
fathom why it sounds like swearing, as you say, finger-pointing, but it
seemed right and I ended it there. The poem concludes with English
people in a hot climate not liking all the flies, but that is, of course, a
figure for involuntary memories that come in disordered, disturbing
bits and pieces. This poem manages to register a few of the problems
that the sequence sets out to externalize — which is where, perhaps,

'From a Memory' gets its other sense: I'm taking glimpses of the past and shaping them into something other than them. The poem is, as you note, from a memory, and not the memory itself.

Perhaps I should think of it the other way round: that these poems shade in some of the words in the later translations we did. Be that as it may, this kinship with Sereni seems to me quite evident, all the more so if some of these poems were written before beginning to read Sereni's. His sense of being ousted from life may have been present in his pre-war writings but, as Franco Fortini says, it was certainly sharpened and deepened by his imprisonment and 'failure' to join the Resistance or take part in history. The backdrop to his Dantesque Algerian Diary is a world conflict. Your sequence has no public setting and so it is harder for it to 'speak for others', be exemplary or emblematic. Sereni would be the first to say he was but one of many and — indeed — says almost precisely this in 'From Holland'. There may be precious little consolation in that, but there may be some. Sereni became the leading poet of the generation after Montale, perhaps because of it. Do you think your poems lack this kind of consolation, as if — as it were — people could feel uninvolved, unimplicated or untouched?

One reviewer in 1988, who spent some time on these poems, described my work as 'love poetry . . . of an exemplary kind.' The problem with that word 'exemplary', though, is that it puts me up on a moral pedestal and suggests that people who want to love or be love poets should be following my example. The very idea is painful.

As for being a leading poet, everything's different, isn't it? The reviewer who in 1983 described me as 'the finest poet of his generation' may have seemed to be making a generous gamble. I have no clear sense that in English poetry there is or has been a leading figure in the generation before mine. There have been a fair number of good English poets. If we take the British Isles and Ireland, then it's conventionally Heaney and Paul Muldoon has occupied that 'leading figure' position for almost two decades.

One reviewer has said that my poems display skill in 'representing natural detail and the way it can seem to bear on our most private and troubled moments'. Given the poems we are discussing, it's to be expected that people would locate their arena, as it were, in private trouble. And as for 'consolation', why does it keep coming up? Poet acquaintances who write in a more abrasively difficult style — where intelligibility itself can be an issue — have talked of the consolations my poems provide in their syntax, forms, rhymes, and the like. I'd be inclined to say that the poems I write attempt to deploy all the means at their disposal to construct counter-weights to the destructive and damaging in experience, but I don't think of those counter-weights as 'consolation'. That's the prize you get when, frankly, you've lost; but the game's not over, we're still playing; and when the game's really over, you don't need art any more anyway. Actually, I would find the burden of being some kind of cultural representative for a generation's sufferings unbearable — and I don't believe that Sereni thought of himself in those terms, or wrote as if he were.

'A September Night' is poised between the 'here and now' of the first verses, and the recalled event, making what goes before a sort of sonnet and what comes after a truncated one (as later in a more evident form in 'For Lavinia').The line 'the livid dark enfolded us' echoes the creases of the first part, and wrenches the word 'lived' into something more sinister. At this line it is far from certain whether we are in a bedroom or elsewhere, reliving the aftermath of the event, whether the September night was then or now. The second half of the poem superimposes itself onto the first, a kind of now structural echoing and jarring.

The final line 'I'd just make amends' has a word you use often. In the next poem, 'we'd just bear' gives it a twist. Earlier, 'until you just forget them' was used in 'From a Memory'. Between the poems the word 'just' is being given twists and turns of meaning, hovering around but never actually leading into a word that is not used in the sequence: justice. Earlier, you said you didn't wait in Milan for the sentence and actually you seem not to have had any interest in 'justice' of that kind at all. A heavy prison sentence (extremely unlikely) would have 'just made amends' or mended nothing at all? This is not a question about your relationship to law courts but about the subject matter of the poems.

Going back for the trial suggests that one or both of us were interested in justice being done, in some sense, but (since the verdict was of no interest) not in punishment being meted out. I suspect that leaving before the verdict and not making inquiries about what it was could also have been a way of cutting off a continuing interest in the 'eye-for-an-eye' aspect of justice. Knowing that, for example, he had got off with a three month suspended sentence might have added fury to the other feelings that were already in place.

I suppose that writing poems about something like this, which couldn't be talked about at the time, suggests the need to give an experience its due, to give its implications and consequences form and, in a sense, reality: to make them objects in the world. That might count as doing justice to what happened in a way that a criminal trial can also function — whatever the outcome — as a way of making the truths in a sequence of events matters of public knowledge. That aspect of justice can take place without a sentence being passed. Perhaps the poems try to do a form of justice to those events and, as such, stand as emblems of reparation, even as they question such a possibility.

Whatever the relation of 'From a Memory' to Sereni, 'The Harm' explicitly alludes to Sereni's poem 'Un incubo' [A Nightmare] in the phrase 'clearly pleasing each other'.

Yes, 'The Harm' was helped along by reading Sereni's poem, but the event it relates is from 1978, before any knowledge of 'Un incubo'. I've found a draft of it that tries to get in the words 'Now others have found a limit / within us': that's an attempted lift which didn't survive. The allusion to Sereni that has stayed in the final poem isn't so directive, more an incidental note, and I'm sure it's there as a form of acknowledgement for the future. There is a debt to be registered. When Emmanuela Tandello made versions of these poems in Italian I asked her simply to render that passage by quoting Sereni's poem in the original.

I'd like to read the word 'arouse' at the end of 'A September Night' and the word 'imperatives' towards the end of 'The Harm', coupled to the word 'awake': arouse not simply as arouse out of sleep, but sexually arouse, and imperatives as sexual orders. The words 'awake' and 'arouse', almost mirror images, have switched over, traded their meanings. In the first poem something delicate is turned into a kind of sexual appetite. In the second, a sexual appetite is expressed as an awakening: a sexualized vocabulary in which what's being denied is the possibility of sexual love, uninterfered with by the nightmare of another event overshadowing it and making it impossible. In Sereni's 'Un incubo' the poet, similarly, overhears others making love, and the sound is like being tortured. In his canon the poem is unusual and, in a sense, inexplicable, almost without context. It registers damage, the inability to feel or ignore others' pleasure and the acute sense of being offended by it, a kind of living death. In your poem the context is much clearer, and the poem is far from mysterious about the living death that is being registered. In a chaste kiss, others are lurking in the background, 'pressing to be near'. Pressing forward and, as it were, replacing the poet, evicting him from his own most intimate experience. The 'incorporated wrong' is wrong-doing made flesh and physically inflicted. But it also seems no less incorporated and suffered in the poet's unsure lips not quite able to press a kiss, merely put 'my lips to yours', no longer able to express passion, driven to distraction about how intimacy could possibly be recomposed or achieved.

The difference between Sereni's poem and mine, like my sequence and Philip Larkin's rape poem 'Deceptions', is that I'm writing about a couple. We're in bed together; and she is also awakened by hearing the other couple making love in the flat upstairs.

The lines from 'Only it startles her so much' to the end of 'Cleaning' are the emotional centre of the sequence. Here nearly all the words resonate across a range of meanings, from 'only' which is not a qualifier, pegging the meaning back, but a way of reinforcing regret, and shadowing in the opposite: if only it didn't startle her. The conclusion of the last line (a summing up of all that has gone before) nonetheless sits uncomfortably, because the directness of such an expression as 'My love' has been deflected, and the poet is left feeling that his own love is also somehow contaminated (as, previously in the colloquialism 'My mistake' where the nature of the mistake, of being mistaken, and mistaking others is crucial to the whole sequence). These possessives and their objects are all in question, aren't they: 'my victim', 'My mistake', 'My love'? I wouldn't want to change a word, but I have an odd point to raise, which maybe you could help me on. The word 'streaming' rather than steaming: it looks absolutely right, but I wouldn't be able to tell you what it means.

'Cleaning' is a poem that surprised me when I wrote it and surprises me still — especially the last line. There's a trace of the grafting youthful maker here and there: 'dispossessed, possessed' looks worked on, and the 'overfaint quiet' is a lift from Sidney's *Apology for Poetry*. But the last seven lines or so: how did I come to get that? As for 'streaming', what I will have had in mind is the effect you get if someone has been almost submerged in bathwater and then suddenly stands up, or when someone is using sponge-fulls of water to rinse their skin. The water is streaming off her upper arm.

'Vacant Possession' picks up from the previous poem's 'dispossessed, possessed'

and turns on a similar contradiction, in the form of an oxymoron. The line that looks to me to give the poem its pivot is 'I'm keeping my proximity', where 'proximity' replaces the diffidence of the colloquial 'distance' but not with a humanly warm, relaxed or intimate word. 'Proximity' is a technical word, entirely in keeping with the technicism of the title, as if, again, we are being given the way words potentially can say so much, but here need to be refined back out of sensitivity. The poem is about a form of over-sensitivity, just as 'Cleaning' contrasts the violence of the cleansing action with the delicacy of the misunderstood touch. The status of the 'keeping' seems to me entirely ambiguous and fraught — an act of generosity that sounds comically like a lie, a way of fulfilling something by recognizing your own solitude, a physical nearness that needs to express itself out of the normal human register and leaves her 'weakly fortress'd from a world of harms'.

Perhaps this is the point where whatever I may have been able to do with this style and this subject matter begins to break down. The poem seems to be about over-sensitivity, about the problem of finding that the world resonates with images of harm: the Sandtex like goosepimpled flesh being one of the 'poor examples', and the only conclusion I could find for this poem was managed a few years after the original drafting when, living in a different house entirely, we were burgled. The ghosted handprint and the muddy soles are adapted from an intrusion of another kind; though people often do feel personally soiled by such house burglaries. In the title 'Vacant Possession' you could feel that the sensitivity to language has become 'over-sensitivity', because the phrase in its house purchasing capacity has been usurped by the rape theme. I thought that the title 'The Counterpane' was too much for that sort of reason, but there the 'pane' and 'pain' pun, which is deployed at the end of 'Vacant Possession' anyway, does feel rudely forced. 'Rudely forced': you can see the problems inherent in analogies here between technique and theme.

'For Lavinia' is a truncated sonnet which cannot finish, but must cut itself off in the recognition that, like Marcus in the play (and maybe in this conversation), too much has been said. Yet there has been precious little saying in the sequence. The couple has exchanged only a few words. 'I concentrated on his tie' is the only direct quote. 'Shall I speak for thee?' is the phrase from Titus Andronicus *that the poem directs its care and outrage against — with its poet who dare not speak for her, and barely dares*

speak at all. Even the little that is said is too much. And this gives the reader, perhaps, an uncomfortable feeling, since, albeit invited, he has trespassed on these poems.

Just last year I was asked to water the plants in a neighbour's flat while they were back in the States, which I did, and the odd thing was that although I'd been invited and had been given a key, going into their empty flat and walking around in it, even to do what they had asked, still felt like a mild trespassing. Why? Perhaps the feeling of trespass is a sign that you are actually respecting someone else's privacy even as you are given an unusual occasion to get a glimpse of it. The reader's position in relation to these poems may well be uneasy, but I can't really see how it could be anything other.

I never thought of 'For Lavinia' as a truncated sonnet; for me, it is a set of quatrains. However, it did have a real lopping off. The poem I wrote had 13 lines: three quatrains and a tie-up last line. When I sent it to the *PN Review*, the editor thought I should cut the last line, and suggested promoting the penultimate to function like that. So I never had a sonnet in mind, but there is a formal sense of something having been brought to a stop, perhaps.

I can't help thinking that 'I've said too much already', which goes dumb and understates the case because the poems have shrieked, is just the right way to end — with all-round trespass. Even the reader, rightly, is rather shunned. Poetry, though, is not something you read, but live with. Presumably for a poet it is something you stand by, too. Do you think the cycle has itself survived? Staying power might make people think about stamina, but the notion of duration is more closely linked to enduring.

Time alone will tell. The earliest one I wrote is only 20 years old this year. I like to think that 'There Again', 'Cleaning', and 'For Lavinia' are among the strongest and most resistant pieces I've written. 'The Harm' and 'A September Night' seem slightly less so, though, for me, the latter's 'I'd only make amends' suggests more about the art of reparation in four words than my critical book *In the Circumstances* in thousands. 'From a Memory' suffers perhaps from being a stuttering start, and 'Vacant Possession' ends in images because it can't find a conclusion. As for enduring: can readers endure them?

Can they take them? Well, I'm not too squeamish about poetry. I don't see why anyone should feel troubled by these poems more than by the things that occur every day in the world. I suspect the problem of reading the poems might come not just from the subject matter, but from gender problems: i.e. a male writer on rape; he can't know anything about it. Or: they can't be about rape. And the poems are not about rape, or knowing anything about it, in fact . . .

I don't wholly follow you here. Only one review of *This Other Life* picked out the sequence for direct criticism of this kind; the *Poetry Review* piece, which I don't have, accused me of re-raping the sequence's 'victim'. Needless to say, I was disturbed by the review, but my wife relieved me from that burden — she being perfectly placed to distinguish between a violent act against a woman and some short lyric poems that very discreetly refer to one. Do you mean to say that the poems really aren't about rape, and don't know about it? Or just that from a fiercely genderist point of view they can't be and I can't know? I could see some justice in the first sense of the sequence as, rather, about circumstantial guilt, agent regret, moral luck, the soil of rape (but not rape itself), reparation, making amends . . . The poems don't have much to say about the rapist, do they?

I meant only that the poems are not about rape in that they are about the consequences of it, and that they do not let their lyricism be sidetracked into psychology 'Why did he do it?', sociology (Nicole Ward Jouve's writings), or a misguided attempt to imagine having another body. And they are not about knowing anything about it, not in the sense that they do not know, but they do not make the knowing something to write about, but to show, in writing. I raised the point only because you mentioned the criticism of the word 'humbling', it having been said that this word reflects more the man's predicament than the woman's — criticism based on the poet 'not understanding' what had happened to the woman. The final verse and appalled conclusion to 'A September Night' seem to me to show a very keen understanding of what had happened to her, to him and to them. No reparation is possible, love becomes an echo of something that certainly was not love.

I owe Nicole Ward Jouve a debt of gratitude: she was my personal tutor at York University, before she had become known as a feminist prose and fiction writer, and encouraged me by, for example, commenting on some juvenilia that I clearly had things to write about but hadn't found how to do it yet. She taught me for a paper on the

French Symbolists, and was (above all) tolerant of my poor French. Later I read her book on the Yorkshire Ripper — after I'd written all the poems in the sequence barring 'For Lavinia'.

In 'The Harm', the 'fat moths rub their bellies' trying to get in. Lurking underneath is the sense of envy, of others more fortunate. But envy is a spoiling feeling, and the sequence works against resignation to it. How is it that so many of the poems appear to end on a note of resignation: 'I'd just make amends', 'My love, this is the dirty thing', 'I've said too much already' yet the overall tone is not one of resignation?

Well, I don't think the poems end on notes of resignation because of the ways in which the forms of utterances can deploy significances quite other than their apparent surface senses. In 'I'd just make amends', the poem's narrated context suggests that this is somehow a lesser thing than, say, happily making love, and it is. The statement is a simple direct assertion at the end of a series of more interwoven statements — so the reader is released into an ambiguous, but directly expressed aim: 'I'm not giving up, though it may sound like it; I'm going to do the best I can.' In 'My love, this is the dirty thing', from 'Cleaning', as you note, the first two words can refer either to my emotion, or can address the object of my emotion. The poem begins 'Seeing as she submerges', so in its course it makes a move from a third person distance to an attempt at a voiced second person relationship. The pronominal shift dramatizes a bid for intimacy that may seem to be denied by the merely descriptive reading of the last line — which refers to emotional damage. Something similar is true for 'I've said too much already', because the line begins with the Shakespearean character's name: 'Lavinia'. In that poem the 'she' is, until the last line, the theatrical character, and the 'you' is my wife. With the last line, I speak to the character as if she were my wife, speak to her as if in the voice of her uncle Marcus. I'm acknowledging in the form of a question to the reader that my words cannot ease her pain, or fathom it, but not letting up on the need to want to do it; I'm leaving the reader with that question: 'And what would I be trying to achieve?' The necessarily impure motives in making art can also be implied. Here, perhaps, the effect is to close the sequence in a falling away that makes an end of the poem, but not of its issues and concerns.

FIVE

The life of a little magazine

NATE DORWARD: *You arrived at Cambridge to do graduate work in 1975. I'd like to hear about that, and about your own interests, projects and expectations at the time. 'In a Tight Corner' from* News for the Ear: A Homage to Roy Fisher *describes how you'd already discovered his work in the social sciences library when you were visiting Bradford in the early 1970s. To what extent were you aware of the current Cambridge poetry scene, and what was it like entering into it?*

I did my first degree at York University. The English Department was largely staffed by Cambridge graduates from the early 60s generations. My supervisor for the three years was the future French feminist writer Nicole Ward Jouve, married to the novelist Anthony Ward — who had been part of the *Prospect* group. He knew Elaine Feinstein, Jeremy Prynne, and Andrew Crozier, and lent me copies of books by the first two. They were Donald Davie students, and I got pointed in the direction of the Black Mountain poets and the Objectivists, so I arrived in Cambridge having read American long poems, Zukofsky, Olson, Dorn, Creeley, as well as Prynne's books up to and including *Brass*, and plenty more besides.

I'd also read some of what were the Fulcrum Press poets, and been most taken with Bunting and Fisher. Because I grew up in the North of England — my father's family in the cities of the Midlands and North West, my mother's from Tyneside with some Scottish relatives — I didn't find it difficult to think of them as poets who were making sense of my particular backgrounds. Though I'd read and absorbed some of the founding materials of 1970s Cambridge poetry, I was already orientated towards a slightly different configuration of the poets who helped change the look of poetry in Britain during the 1960s. There was a girl at York, for instance, with whom I was to be briefly romantically involved, who had grown up in Glasgow. She was a fan of Ian Hamilton Finlay and Edwin Morgan.

Ezra Pound died during my three years at York and there was a good deal of interest in him. I'd long been absorbed in painting and the visual arts (my first idea was to go to Art School) and at York I did a special paper on some art history topics. I didn't think of myself as a graduate student, didn't even think I'd do well enough in the Finals exams, and so decided to take a year off, and see what happened. The most decisive and devastating thing that happened is the Italian rape which I've written and talked about elsewhere. Well, despite my self-doubts, I got a First, was undecided about what to do, applied to Oxford, Cambridge, and the Courtauld Institute, London. Oxford wasn't interested, but the other two interviewed me and both said OK. In the end I decided to go to Cambridge, with the idea that I would do a PhD on Pound and the Visual Arts. There was nothing much on the subject back then. What I ended up discovering about the topic eventually emerged in my part of the 1985 book published by the Tate Gallery, *Pound's Artists*. By then I'd long given up that line, changed to something on Davie, Tomlinson, Fisher, and Larkin, and been awarded the doctorate in the early 1980s. Looking back, the extraordinary thing is that I was able to do anything at all on a poet like Fisher who was still in his forties when I started work on it.

How did you get involved in starting up and editing Perfect Bound?

I made contact with a group called the Cambridge Poetry Society. Its members were not only undergraduates. It was one of the contexts in which tentative town/gown collaborations might occur. They ran a weekly poetry workshop, edited an annual magazine called *Blueprint*, and organized a weekly reading by an invited poet. The funds to do that came from three sources: the Cambridge English Faculty, the Eastern Arts Association, and the National Poetry Secretariat (attached to the Poetry Society in London). To qualify for the first of these we needed a faculty member as our senior treasurer. That was Jeremy Prynne. At the Eastern Arts was a very positive young woman called Irene McDonald. It must have been she who indicated to the committee of the society that there might be funds available if we wanted to set up a real little magazine.

The name *Perfect Bound*, taken from the printer's specification of course, was alighted on by Bill Bennett. The nature of the magazine as it evolved was to a large extent determined by the fact that we were given a grant large enough to publish 88 pages about twice a year. As you know, it's quite hard to keep doing that on a regular basis without a professional structure. At the same time, it was supposed to be a magazine of the Cambridge Poetry Society, so we published pieces by students, some work by people who came and read, contributions from local poets (and there were quite a few in the town), and material by people we solicited directly. It was one of my great regrets that Roy Fisher never seemed to have anything he could spare. Soon people started approaching us too.

But it's worth underlining the social context in which the magazine arose and how it was supported, because although — being a graduate student with more time at my own disposal — I ended up editing all the issues (with a series of co-editors from the society), the magazine was not my personal plaything, and was not edited with the single-minded aim of promoting my vision of poetry at that date. I was still learning as much as I could and as fast as possible, and didn't have a vision of poetry aside from the developing one I needed for my own work, and I've never thought that the personal one had to be pushed as the only one. So the heterogeneous nature of the magazine's contextual support coincided to some extent with my sense of a distinction to be maintained between all the various things that were happening, and my private take on them. Even in the schoolyard I was never much of a gang-member, and, one way or another, I've stayed that way.

Could you tell me a bit about the Cambridge Poetry Festivals, and their impact on the magazine?

The life of *Perfect Bound* was marked clearly by the Festival in 1975 run by Richard Burns, the one in 1977 run by Paul Johnstone, and the one in 1979 run by me. The 1975 one, which took place in April, was already legendary by the time I reached Cambridge in early October. It helped to create the mood of something happening which probably encouraged Eastern Arts to think that sponsoring a magazine might not be a bad idea. The event had been overshadowed by the deaths immediately after it of Rolf Dieter Brinkmann and Veronica Forrest-Thomson. My first ever published book review in issue one was written from a copy of the typescript of her *On the Periphery*. Johnstone's festival, for which I worked as the secretary, was like a forerunner of the more recent experimentalist conferences, except that unlike them it was organized to be like Burns's — with international airfares and other high expenses, requiring the making of a lot of money from ticket sales. The latter didn't happen and the society was badly in debt when I was invited to take it over.

The policy of my festival — run in close collaboration with a brilliant treasurer called Alison Rimmer who worked for Heffers Bookshop — was again a combination of principle and pragmatism. We needed to get out of debt. Hence the big Saturday Night event with Allen Ginsberg, Anne Waldman and Kenneth Koch. Ginsberg did the whole thing for a tiny fee plus flights on to his next festival. The idea was to present the widest range of poetries so as to attract as many constituencies as possible. There was an afternoon of Sound Poetry, a debate between Silkin and Davie about poetry and politics, big readings by Hans Magnus Enzensberger and Joseph Brodsky, Edmond Jabès with Rosemary Waldrop translating, Michael Hamburger talking about Celan with an exhibition of his French wife's etchings . . . We turned a big deficit into a modest profit. The main drawback was that trying to please everybody we ended up offending quite a lot of the splendid-isolationist cliques.

There were some people for whom the pluralism was just a bit too much, of course. I vividly recall CH Sisson getting up and walking out as Ginsberg launched into a sort-of-sung version of Blake's 'Nurse's Song'. Well, that festival is one of the things I can feel did make a statement . . . a bit before its time, perhaps. Mrs Thatcher had just won her first term, and we were in for a general hardening and factionalizing in the whole society, with a concomitant travestying of the realities of the factionalized groups. Yet the stress of organizing the 1979 festival, of editing the magazine, of trying to finish my doctorate, get launched as a publishing writer, and live a life — was just too much. I staggered into the Thatcher era without a job, with a PhD to resubmit, and with some disillusionments about the extent to which poets and writers could be expected to collaborate under a Popular Front kind of cultural banner. I stopped doing the magazine and handed the festival on to other people.

All seven issues list you as a co-editor with a number of other people. Could you give me an account of the shifts of editorship in the journal's life?

To my mind, the magazine's life divides into three parts. The first two issues were edited by 'Bill Bennett & Peter Robinson', as it says; the third, fourth and fifth were edited by Peter Robinson and Aidan Semmens, though the third still names Bennett as an editor, and the final two were edited by Peter Robinson with Richard Hammersley. In the first two I was finding my feet and taking instruction from the other editor — who showed me how the golf-ball typewriter worked and how the paste-up was done (overnight sittings with coffee and the fumes from the glue to keep us going). The middle three were edited harmoniously and enthusiastically, with improvements in the production values that probably peaked with issue five, and a consensus, more or less, about what we were publishing. The final two issues show a certain restlessness with that consensus and an attempt to widen the catchment area of the contributions.

I'm not familiar with the names of your co-editors outside the pages of Perfect Bound — *could you tell me a little about them?*

Only a little, I'm afraid. Richard Hammersley was a graduate student in experimental psychology from Glasgow. I lost touch with him soon after the magazine editing stopped. He has pursued an academic career. Bill Bennett was a survivor of Cambridge's communes and squats period. He lived in a derelict property in what was the Kite area before its demolition. He was not a very reliable co-editor and in the end I got tired of trying. I've no idea what his fate has been. Aidan Semmens made contact again quite recently thanks to Richard Caddel. He edited one or two issues of another small magazine called *Molly Bloom* after graduating. He works as a sub-editor and journalist, now, living in Suffolk.

Since I'm sure many readers won't have seen the run of Perfect Bound, *perhaps you could give me a tour through the issues and the selections in them that now stand out for you the most.*

Each of the issues contains work still of interest, I believe, some of it finding its way into individual collections at later dates. Issue One opened our account with 'The Land of Saint Martin' by J. H. Prynne. Then come two sections from 'The Art of Flight' by Allen Fisher, poems about the burning of the Crystal Palace that I was very taken by. Then, picking out some things, there's a run of work by first-year graduate student poets: my poem 'World's Apart' which will come first in a future *Selected Poems*, 'Six Days' by Geoffrey Ward, and 'Driving Each Other' by John Wilkinson; there are six poems by Edwin Morgan, and 'After Christopher Wood' by John James. The reviews section contains pieces by Semmens on McClure, Ward on Dorn's *Gunslinger*, myself on Veronica Forrest-Thomson's *On the Periphery*, and Wilkinson on Crozier's *Residing*.

Issue Two follows this pattern with a special feature on Tom Raworth gathered and edited by Geoffrey Ward: a section from *Writing*, some poems from *Common Sense* including one called 'Magnetic Water' I particularly like, and a piece on the poet by Ward. Denise Levertov had given a reading. We wrote to her and she sent a sequence called 'Metamorphic Journal'. John Matthias was, by pure chance, living all but next door to me in Herschel Road and he gave us 'After the Death of Chekhov'. There's more work by the graduate students, this time including parts of Rod Mengham's *Beds and Scrapings*, plus an undergraduate poem of some refinement, 'The Novel Detective' by Adam Clarke-Williams. There's a review of George Oppen's *Collected Poems* by Chris Hunt, and of Roy Fisher's *Nineteen Poems and an Interview* by me.

Issue Three is one of my favourites: five poems — one of which was recently included in Keith Tuma's Oxford *Anthology of Twentieth Century British and Irish Poetry* — by Christopher Middleton (who had read for us), 'Old Bosham Bird Watch' by Lee Harwood, another interesting poem by Clarke-Williams, some prose poems by Ken Smith, Iain Sinclair's 'The Horse. The Man. The Talking Head (a Note on Howard Hughes)', a piece of Beckettian prose by Marcus Perryman, three poems by Gael Turnbull, five poems by Matthew Mead, more *Writing* by Raworth, plus poems by the regulars including John Wilkinson's 'Political Health' and Aidan Semmens's 'The Strange Geometry' — which won the Chancellor's Medal for a poem by an undergraduate in 1977. There are two reviews of Turnbull by Clarke-Williams and Perryman, and a piece on Mark Hyatt by Wilkinson. The production values take a leap forward.

That's indeed an interesting poem by Adam Clarke-Williams — 'The Ambassadors: Raymond Williams in Cambridge, Christmas in Portsmouth' — a long title and some striking lines: 'your increment of pleasure gone haywire'; 'the crystals of shifting hungers'. Perhaps you could tell me something about him and about Perryman — two regular contributors to Perfect Bound*'s poetry and review pages who don't seem to have published much outside the journal.*

Adam Clarke-Williams was an extremely scrupulous undergraduate poet who didn't appear to be writing for any of the juvenile self-expression reasons. He published a pamphlet of just eight poems called *Programme Notes* with Richard Tabor's Lobby Press in 1978. Many of them had first appeared in *Perfect Bound*. He became a journalist too, and now works behind the scenes for the BBC. He's remained a friend and continues to write poetry, but doesn't publish. What seems to have happened is that, once out of Cambridge, his sense of a style to write in or a project to develop lost its focus. I think you can see it happening in the poems that appear in the last two issues of the magazine. He soon lost faith in the small press endeavour — at least as far as his own work is concerned — and went through a long phase of trying to write in a more congenial style, but, since he doesn't publish, few people know of the results. We're still in contact and meet every so often.

Marcus Perryman moved to Italy immediately after graduating and lives and works in Verona as a professional translator. He was my brother-in-law for a brief period in the late 1980s. We're in almost daily e-mail contact because together we've translated the complete poems of Vittorio Sereni (our *Selected Poems of Vittorio Sereni* appeared from Anvil in 1990). He continued to write — but not publish — up until a few years ago; now he seems to have turned his creative attentions entirely to playing chess. He's one of my best and most lucid critics. A few years ago we did some e-mail conversations, a couple of which appeared in internet magazines. There's one in *The Cortland Review*, for instance, on the poems about a rape from *This Other Life*.

Let's return to the second 'phase' of the journal. Can you say a bit about the next issue, number four?

Issue Four opens with the short 'Opus Number' by Harry Guest, followed by the wonderful 'Untitled Sequence' by Peter Riley, then poems by John Welch, Richard Caddel, myself, Gael Turnbull, Michael Haslam, Ian Patterson, Nick Totton, Tim Dooley, more *Writing*, two poems by Matthew Mead, the lovely 'Jane Welch's Wedding Testament' by Augustus Young, more prose from Perryman, another interesting piece from Clarke-Williams, an uncollected poem by Douglas Oliver called 'Fun House' and a sequence by Ken Smith called 'Fun City Winter'. There's a piece of uncollected prose by F.T. Prince about the composition of his 'Afterword on Rupert Brooke', a review by Peter Riley of *Science and Society in Prehistoric Britain* by E. W. MacKie, and two reviews which struck a new note: Lee Harwood was not happy with the tone of Semmens's review of *Old Bosham Bird Watch*, and Denise Riley detected some sexist patronizing in my piece on her *Marxism for Infants*. I was surprised and upset.

I do note that Perfect Bound, *like most poetry journals of the 1960s and 1970s, was heavily tilted towards male authors . . . in the issue with your review of that book of Riley's, for instance, there are no female contributors at all. This was pretty typical of avant-garde-oriented journals of the period* — The English Intelligencer *for instance in its hundreds and hundreds of pages only published work by three female authors (Feinstein, Vickers and Mulford). I'm sure this is one of the few aspects of* Perfect Bound *that you must be less than happy about in retrospect. Could you comment on this gender imbalance — its origins, the extent to which it concerned you at the time, and its relationship to matters of poetics? One sometimes comes across the conventional idea that because avant-garde poetries are in the business of destabilizing identity, they are therefore unsuited to the feminist recovery of women's voices and experiences. That's a stark opposition that recent critics like Clair Wills or Romana Huk have tried to complicate . . .*

There were some local considerations: Cambridge still had single-sex colleges, and only three for women. The poetry society had hardly any women members! I don't ever recall us rejecting poems by women authors. The occasion didn't arise. If Veronica Forrest-Thomson had been alive, I'm sure we would have asked her to contribute, and my third published review was of Denise Riley's first pamphlet. There's also some effort being made in the last three issues to have some poetry by women. Yes, it was a bad situation, and we weren't taking many active steps to change it.

Given that the magazine was experimentalist in its general leanings, there was also the problem of finding women writers who would fit the bill. The prominence of Denise Levertov in issue two indicates how much she constituted a sort of rare ideal. Elaine Feinstein, with her early connections to Olson and later ones to Russian avant gardes, was thought by some to be not quite experimental enough. Publishing her 'Two Poems from an "England Sequence"' in issue seven was, in local terms, making a stand against that over-restrictive definition. I would also have to admit that we weren't really concerned with the gender balance in ways that would soon become a proper necessity.

As to the relation of feminism to avant-garde poetics, I think it's too complex an issue to be discussed in such terms in an interview of this kind. There would be, for instance, the problem for me that definitions of avant-garde writing as 'destabilizing identity' would need qualification. It's certainly the case that this sort of slogan was what got put on various strategies then and for years to come. Actually, I found myself growing more and more out of sympathy with this notion of what serious poets were meant to be about. Were they really destabilizing their own? It was supposed to be political, but where I grew up there were all sorts of social and personal problems, with political implications, that came from people having rather weak identities that were being fiercely buffeted by their social circumstances. I never felt myself in possession of one of the anathematized subjectivities that needed destabilizing, rather with masses of conflictual and contradictory experience and hurt that needed putting together and making sense of — and perhaps that's one of the more personal reasons why I started to move away.

I think writers of an experimentalist or modernist bent would say that they have found such techniques essential for dealing with 'conflictual and contradictory experience and hurt', kinds of experience which more conventional approaches might be incapable of dealing with accountably.

You're right, they would, and they'd have good arguments. But my early poems, the ones I'm thinking of, some of which appeared in issues three and four, have an evasively joky manner, and take an allusive glance at damage without being able to address it. I just felt that it wasn't a promising way for me to continue.

Back to Perfect Bound: *tell me about issue five, which you've said concludes the magazine's second phase.*

Issue Five, which looks the best, is perhaps slightly flat in terms of content: a piece of prose and a poem by John Riley (which must have been among the last publications in his cut-short lifetime), work by Thomas A. Clark, Paul Green, two more good poems by Clarke-Williams, Turnbull, Perryman, David Chaloner, Mengham, Wendy Mulford's 'Chinese Postcard Sequence', a section from part two of 'Suicide Bridge' by Iain Sinclair . . . Yet, despite this slight air of a repeat performance in a well worked theme, the issue does contain one of Jeremy Prynne's rare ventures into critical prose: 'Reader's Lockjaw', a review of books by Paul St. Vincent (soon to be revealed as E. A. Markham).

I'd always wondered about that review — whether Prynne had known that St. Vincent was a pseudonym (actually heteronym) when he wrote it. I take it he wasn't, to your knowledge? — Perhaps you could say a little more about

Prynne's influence at the time on Perfect Bound *and the Cambridge poetry scene more generally.*

We felt very honoured to be offered that piece, and I vividly recall Jeremy Prynne visiting my flat opposite St John's College in order to correct the phrase 'prostrate operation' into 'prostate operation'. Doubtless, he was living in fear of the kinds of misprints that we were only too prone to making. But, as I say, that issue was the best produced of the set. No, I don't think he knew who the author was at the time he wrote the review. I'd come across the Lambchops poems in one or two small magazines, magazines that also contained poems by E. A. Markham. I found the St. Vincent poems vivid and seriously funny, and kept up with Markham's work through three large Anvil Press collections.

Since the example of Jeremy's poetry and outlook was having an evident influence on John Wilkinson's rapidly evolving work, his seemed a game that couldn't be played by anyone else. I had tried imitating the style of *Kitchen Poems* in 1973, but was so completely unconvinced by the results that I kept away later. Nevertheless, I read three of his books closely and repeatedly: *Kitchen Poems, The White Stones,* and *Brass.* Some of his global political vision and the way he brought that back home to the kitchen sink, and the human body, its wounds and responses, in work of that period went in deeply.

His influence on the magazine is hard to calculate. He kept a respectful distance and didn't push a line of poets at us. It came more indirectly via suggestions from others, I think. He used to attend some of the readings we organized and, again, was careful not to push himself forward, but would sometimes have a quiet word with the poets after the readings. Perhaps he felt this was part of his duty as the society's senior treasurer. On the other hand, he never had anything whatsoever to do with the Cambridge Poetry Festival, so his absence from the later experimental conferences is not surprising.

Another thing to bear in mind about his influence is that Adam Clarke-Williams had a large collection of poetry from the entire spectrum of Fifties, Sixties and Seventies experiment. He had the collected poems of Edwin Denby, for instance. He had that collaboration between Tom Phillips, John James, and Andrew Crozier. Coming from the South coast, he was a fan of Lee Harwood's writings. He had *Some Trees* and *The Tennis Court Oath* — when Ashbery's early work was very difficult to find in the UK. So the material that was going into the student idea of Cambridge poetry at that date was by no means drawing only upon the writers associated with the older poets from Cambridge. However, while Jeremy Prynne was a frighteningly articulate presence, he wasn't unapproachable or forbidding when approached. He was, strange as it may seem, the human face of the Cambridge avant garde — and he supported me during many difficult years with regular college teaching and long, long late night literary conversations. It was his advice, too, which partly helped indirectly to precipitate me into my present much happier situation.

Prynne's prose writings are comparatively rare: letters made public, a handful of reviews, several talks and lectures, and a recent publication on Shakespeare's 94th sonnet. This is a strikingly small body of prose writing for someone who is, besides a major poet, a dedicated scholar and teacher. One might say the same thing of Andrew Crozier, too, whose only book-length scholarly publications are the recent editions of Rakosi and Rodker. The comparative scarcity of manifestos, critical prose, commentaries, &c was commented upon polemically by Drew Milne in the pages of Parataxis, *for whom it's part of a general 'agoraphobia': 'the seemingly patrician reluctance of small-press poets to write prose commentary on their own work or on others'. Does this seem to you an inaccurate or unduly harsh characterization of the attitudes towards extra-poetic writing in the small-press scene of the time? Would you be able to comment on the sources of the reluctance that Milne's describing?*

The most authentically patrician of twentieth-century Cambridge poets, Sir William Empson (the son of a Yorkshire landowner), was — as John Haffenden's recent edition of *The Complete Poems* makes amply clear — quite willing to explicate and comment on his own work. On the other hand, Ludwig Wittgenstein (son of a very wealthy Viennese industrialist), who has had an unusually sustained influence on poets, wrote and taught at Cambridge for longish periods while publishing almost nothing at all. Those two examples give you a broad range of possibilities. More recently, Donald Davie, who has a good claim to being a father figure of the present Cambridge School (whether from being followed or resisted), may have suffered in his reputation as a poet *because* he wrote so much criticism. Perhaps the reluctance of Cambridge poets from Tomlinson through the Prynne generation to put out books of criticism may have something to do with wanting to avoid the Davie pitfall and survive in the academy without succumbing to the criticism industry — thus being known as poets, pure if not simple. Benjamin Jowett once said that 'Gentlemen never explain', and the 'seeming-patrician' air might be attributable to ways that meritocracy boys learnt to camouflage themselves in a still patrician environment. Davie's essay 'Remembering the Movement' is clear-sighted about problems associated with over-cultivating the reader in poems, and the same notions might well have reverberated in a reluctance to court them in occasional prose too.

Then there's a socio-historical reason. When Empson was writing his epoch-making critical books, there weren't many academic jobs around and criticism was, thanks to T. S. Eliot perhaps, oddly fashionable — but he ended up in first Japan, then China. Davie needed to make an academic name fast in the post-war period, when the criticism vogue was still going, so as to support a family. The university expansion programme of the early sixties meant that people of the Prynne generation (such as those who taught me in York) could get jobs on the basis of a good Oxbridge BA and a reference. That little golden age of non-publishers was coming to an end in the 1970s, and absolutely evaporated in the Thatcher era with first the university cuts, and then the establishment of the research assessment business where university departments have to field a first team of scribbling-publishing players. It's perhaps worth noting too that in books like *Some Versions of Pastoral* or *Articulate Energy* the division between the academic and non-academic is far less like an iron curtain. Those books are not big on footnotes and academic apparatus. They are aimed at a generally well-informed reader.

You said that the magazine began to shift with the last two issues. Could you describe that final pair?

Issue Six begins with substantial translations by Stephen Romer of Jacques Dupin. There are also a few of my translations of Pierre Reverdy, of Philippe Jacottet by Tim Dooley, and of Alain Delahaye by Michael Edwards. There are translations of Nasos Vayenas, Yunna Morits, August Graf von Hallermünde, Yevtushenko, Pirandello, and Margarite Aliger. So it almost looks like the translation issue. But then there is, for instance, 'Digest of the Poetical Works of Dora Oliver' by Peter Riley, 'It's my Town (But I had to Leave It)' by Geoffrey Ward, work by Charles Tomlinson, John Welch, Denise Riley, and Edwin Morgan . . . Plus an unusually interesting prose piece called 'from

Studio 38' by Richard Bentley, an undergraduate. There's a review of Geoffrey Hill's *Tenebrae* by Eric Griffiths, and Wilkinson on books by Nigel Wheale and Geoffrey Ward.

Issue Seven is the one designed to represent what was happening at the 1979 Poetry Festival as well as to continue business as usual: so Enzensberger, Christoph Meckel, Edmond Jabès, Michel Deguy, and Anne Waldman rub shoulders with Elaine Feinstein's 'Two Lyrics from "An England Sequence"', Denise Riley, Mead, Raworth, a distinctive student poem by A. T. Tribble called 'An Appeal for Nakedness at Funerals and on Occasions of Great National Mourning', 'A Lyrical Ballad' by John Barrell, plus other translations and poems by the regulars, such as Marcus Perryman's untitled prose poem 'On the floor . . .' But there is also a feeling that the magazine may be losing its focus. The volume has opened itself up to a vast area of poetry in English and in translation, but doesn't have a policy for deciding how to construct a coherent issue.

For me, the magazine had probably outgrown its usefulness. While issues one, two and five contain poems that went into *Overdrawn Account*, published by John Welch in 1980, and three and four have poems that went into a pamphlet called *A Part of Rosemary Laxton* (1979), issue six contains my poem 'Looking Up' and seven has other poems which were to find their way some ten years later into my first Carcanet book, *This Other Life*. It was during 1978 that I started to write the poems that seem fully to strike my own note. By the end of the decade, I was moving away from an uneasy alliance with what has come to be called Cambridge school poetry and into as much of the entire field full of folk as I can manage to live with and appreciate.

I want to return for a moment to your comment earlier about your allergy to literary gangs. It reminded me that I've never, in fact, talked to a poet who felt comfortable with being labeled part of a school or movement, even though such terms seem to be unavoidable in the stories we tell ourselves about literary history, and especially about modern poetry for some reason. Peter Riley, asked by Kelvin Corcoran in a 1983 interview 'Is there a "Cambridge" group of poets?' memorably prefaced his reply 'Well, there was, and wasn't, and there isn't'. I think, also, of Crozier and Longville's obviously careful choice of the title A Various Art. *Furthermore, there are complications created by the longevity of groupings — Riley's 'isn't' suggests that he sees the work of later writers like Wilkinson, Mengham, &c as being distinct from the 1960s group around* The English Intelligencer *and Grosseteste*

Review. *Does the term 'Cambridge school' make sense to you, and if so how do you use it?*

There's a Wittgenstein anecdote from the 1930s where a young Theodore Redpath tells the philosopher that he's just bought some classical records, and Wittgenstein asks 'Are they any good?' Redpath, trying to be subtle, replies: 'It depends what you mean by "good".' And back comes Wittgenstein: '*I* mean what *you* mean.'

So, the term 'Cambridge school' means to me what you mean by it: it's an elastic term stretching from a fairly loose affiliation of avant-garde poetries, to an inner circle of J. H. Prynne plus a few friends. It works to exclude poets who have perfectly good claims to be Cambridge poets, like Clive Wilmer, but who are rightly taken not to be Cambridge school poets, and of course it can exclude poets who passed through the town as undergraduates such as Michael Hofmann. How do I prefer to use it? I don't. Hardly anyone who appears to belong to it likes the term, and some of those who don't belong seem to resent it. So I prefer to keep clear of the whole idea.

What I would prefer would be an extension of the history to pre-Prynne decades, a more perspicuous survey of what has happened in the town since the founding of the Cambridge English School — you know, less pigeon holes and more complex descriptions.

Yes, that's what Peter Riley would like too, I think — I seem to recall his once even suggesting that any such survey would have to reach back to the 17th-century Cambridge Platonists!

Fair enough.

One thing that surprised me, looking over Perfect Bound *again, was that its contributions drew on a wider spectrum of the UK avant garde of the time than I remembered — there are a few authors I miss, like Bill Griffiths, Barry MacSweeney and Bob Cobbing, which suggests it had a different flavour from Eric Mottram's* Poetry Review, *but on the other hand one of the magazine's most frequent contributors was Allen Fisher, another of Mottram's favourites. Nonetheless, I think it would be fair to say that the journal, along with the contemporary issues of* Grosseteste Review, *performed an important function in reworking or consolidating a 'Cambridge School', and a lot of early work by Wilkinson, Mengham, Ward, et al — what might now be considered a second poetic generation — first appeared in its pages. Could you comment on the role you feel the journal played in the development of this particular strand of experimental writing?*

Well, it's also probably the case that these younger writers were, let's say, under-age volunteers for the forward positions. They weren't recruited, they had to get themselves acknowledged as such. And there was, I believe, some friction between the generations: note the absence of Wilkinson and his friends from *A Various Art*. They were the young poets of Cambridge when I arrived, and my role looks retrospectively rather like providing them with a platform — something which may have got taken for granted. I still have a typed letter from John Wilkinson, then in Harvard, warning me about what he calls a major and undesirable shift in my editorial policy. I had dared to ask for some cuts to a piece of Geoff's on Rod's work. This was characterized as censorship, the piece was withdrawn, and never appeared in *Perfect Bound*.

Mind you, I remember feeling much worse when in the late Seventies it became clear that a loose affiliation of Oxford-based writers had taken over the metropolitan power base. I'm referring to the Martians and the so-called new narrative poets. All these years later, Raine's 'revolution' has come to look, I suspect, like an episode in the history of publicity — while Motion's social ambitions have resulted in his shunting himself into the most creatively-damaging job a poet could wish for: the Laureateship. But back then it was possible to think that some well-placed, but only moderately talented people had hijacked the future.

Indeed! Let me quote a little from Motion and Morrison's preface to their 1982 Penguin Book of Contemporary British Poetry: *there they talk of 'a stretch, occupying much of the 1960s and 70s, when very little — in England at any rate — seemed to be happening, when achievements in British poetry were overshadowed by those in drama and fiction, and when, despite the presence of strong individual writers, there was a lack of overall shape and direction.' From a different angle, of course, plenty was happening in UK poetry, from the prolific burst of avant-garde-affiliated poetries (*The White Stones, Moving, Place, Tracts of the Country, Pleats, *Roy Fisher's collected poems) to the appearance of new books by older figures like Jones, Graham, Middleton, Prince and Bunting, to major volumes by 'established' poets like Geoffrey Hill (*Mercian Hymns). *Would you have some thoughts on how erasures of the historical record such as Motion and*

Morrison's ended up taking place? I'd also like to know your own take on the history of this period.

I appeared on a panel with Motion and Morrison at the ICA in the year that their anthology came out. Michael Horovitz, editor of *Children of Albion* — an anthology of 1960s experiment (also from Penguin), was in the audience. There was a heated series of exchanges in which I managed to get Morrison to acknowledge that comments in their poorly-written introduction about the absence of anthologies between Alvarez and their own was a misleading travesty of the record. But then their anthology was never intended to be a serious attempt at a historical account. It's an old-style take-over bid based on the fact that London has a large population and only a few literary periodicals and papers. By taking over some editorial chairs in publishing houses and literary journals, then selling your chosen wares to the metropolis, you can (for a while) kid yourself that you are determining the shape of literary history. Cultures are much more complex than that, though, and those two Ms are already being filed by time and change closer to their proper worth.

Summary dismissal is the preferred way of the powerful; so I don't see any difficulty in understanding how they might like to pretend that the 1960s and 1970s experimental development more or less never happened. However, I would say that their attempt to keep Geoffrey Hill out of the picture was ignorant even on their own terms. After all, as is well documented and acknowledged by Heaney, *Mercian Hymns* stopped him in his experiments with the prose poem in *Stations* and had a decided influence on the 'word-hoard' poems of *North*. Heaney paid his respects to the work in 'Englands of the Mind' too. The inclusion of Jeffrey Wainwright in their anthology was nice to see at the time, but that too (given Wainwright's evident 'school of Hill' credentials) made the attempt to sideline the poet of *King Log* and *Mercian Hymns* look ill-conceived.

It's not really possible for me to give a thumbnail sketch of Seventies poetry in Britain. There was far too much going on and I was just trying to find out about it. There were many more magazines than now, many of the very short-lived variety. There were lots of little presses that could produce good-looking books quite cheaply. John Welch's Many Press, for instance, was never more than a basement or attic venture with an occasional grant to do a slightly more substantial volume, like my first collection, but he published many people who are still writing strongly. The 1960s and the idea of underground culture had meant that there was no simple rule for dismissing a book on the basis of its publisher's name. There were both specialist poetry bookshops and general bookshops in university towns with reasonable poetry sections. Most of this has disappeared. I think that poetry then seemed a very lively thing to be involved with, something that mattered a lot, and a field that was populated by valuable writers of various older generations who were to be respected and learned from. I was lucky enough to meet a few of them, who proved generous and supportive of the young as well.

That anthology of Motion and Morrison succeeded in re-establishing the rather tenuous notion of a metropolitan literary establishment, and in establishing the two Ms as a couple of smart-ish operators. It helped to inaugurate two decades (so far) of unhistorical misinformation in the guise of bringing poetry to the people. But the sales of poetry books and the almost total withdrawal of general publishers from poetry during the same period have given that the lie.

You ask how it happened that this kind of forgetting took place? There's a lot of other cultural forgetting that I would want to counteract. At the heart of it somewhere is a sense that, speaking very generally, in Britain both the pillars of the academy and the literary journalists didn't have that much time for contemporary poetry, and didn't care much whether true accounts were given of it or not. Matters may be even worse now. Poetry, even of the 'popular' varieties, seems to have been more or less abandoned by the media and, while there are plenty of creative writing schools, the academic legitimacy of contemporary poetry may not have got that much farther than when I was wrote some PhD chapters on Roy Fisher.

Andrew Duncan, in the preface to Angel Exhaust 8, *says of you: 'once an editor of* Perfect Bound, *in the heart of Cambridge poetry, he is now a completely mainstream poet, never straying by a syllable'. I can imagine that you'll want to contest that rather loaded description, but certainly your career and writing have taken unusual paths for someone at one point closely involved in 1970s non-mainstream and avant-garde poetries. It's a career that can't be sketched out here at length, but let me just quickly note your association with Carcanet Press, your scholarly work on Geoffrey Hill, and your co-editing of the 1980s journal* Numbers, *all associations with what might be characterized as a formally conservative though modernist-*

inflected mainstream. But I would like to know a little more about your shift indirection.

One way it was marked was by the appearance in 1978 of a broadside of yours from the Many Press, your poem called 'Going Out to Vote' — for John Wilkinson. The dedication has an edge: the poem ends, 'My word, but you do go on.' In response to an interviewer's comment in 1992 about the demands his poetry places on the reader, Wilkinson quoted your line from memory and added 'I'm prepared to accept that with pride!' Could you say a little about this poem, and more generally about the shift in your career and writing at this point?

Well, you know, I don't have a 'career' as a poet: so that hasn't shifted. I have a compulsion, a habit, a vocation if you like. I have a precarious and marginal career as a university literature teacher — who now, in middle age, is able to bank some kudos from also publishing poetry. The poem for John Wilkinson was written in the early summer of 1977. It's my most sustained single piece, the one in which it's me who's going on (the last line being obviously self-referential too) — about a cultural predicament and a loss of confidence in the way that some of my contemporaries were going about responding to it. One of the things that happened next is I wrote a poem in 1978 called 'In the Background Details' (which appeared in *Overdrawn Account*) and more recently, lightly revised, in the *Liverpool Accents* anthology as 'In the Background'. I like it, and will put it into the *Selected Poems*. It's an attempt to write a landscape description from shifting viewpoints, without any located or implied consciousness.

But there are phrases like 'your mother' in it, and there was to be a memory of my father preaching on the back of a lorry that just would not fit at all. A couple of years later I started writing another longish one called 'A Short History' (in *This Other Life* and *Liverpool Accents*) which started up from this apparently unusable fragment about my dad preaching. I had subject matter — my provincial family background, the social and historical circumstances of my difficult love relationship, and not least the Italian rape — that demanded to be written about in ways which would be understandable to people who were not poetry experts — my mother and father, for instance.

What was John Wilkinson's response to 'Going Out to Vote'?

John was evidently stung by the poem. He wrote a fiercely sarcastic

'Note from the Sponsor' about it, which I still have, and he could recall, more or less, its last line over a decade later. Well, I'm sorry about the hurt now. But I don't think I could possibly have written it without a certain animus. What's worse, John is being set up — I'm afraid — as an occasion for a more general consideration of problems about the situation of the young and advanced poet that he exemplified for me back then in a very stark way. 'Going Out to Vote' is a survey of the territory of such a poet's relationship to social, cultural and historical knowledge: who sponsors this figure? What relation does this poet have to inherited wealth? From where does the special access to insight derive? Who was he, or less often she, addressing? What use is a poem's apparent moral or political correctness in lived historical situations? Things of that sort.

So how would you qualify Duncan's version of your position?

Andrew Duncan's mischaracterization of me comes to this: I was never in the heart of the Cambridge school, because to be in the heart of something you have to be taken to heart, and that didn't happen. Moreover, I have never been a part of the mainstream, because aside from a small and fluctuating group of people who promote each other in or via the Metropolis, I don't think there is a mainstream. There are just lots of people who don't get allowed into the more forward echelons of the avant garde, or into that nebulous metropolitan conspiracy. These others publish where they can, try to build up a readership which is larger than their expanded address books, hope that they'll get reviewed, and that their books will sell in reasonable enough numbers for the publisher to think it worth putting out a next one. They rarely win prizes, don't get invited to read at festivals, are not often the subject of specialist articles, and work somewhere in the penumbra between the small metropolitan in-crowd, and total obscurity. I've been fairly lucky, and hardworking — and as a result, I'm in that half-light. But to call this the mainstream is neither to understand my poetry, nor to have read it with much care — nor to care about having better descriptions of a culture than that crudest of us/them binarisms.

I partly moved away because I could no longer credit the identification of what may be innovative formalisms with advanced politics. I don't, for example, think that the poetry I have to write is in any sense formally conservative. I don't call rhyming or having prose syntax or having stanzas, or using the stress-timed metres of spoken English, or using the varied line lengths of the English pindaric, or of free-verse for that matter, or syllabics (all of which I can and have used) either conservative or radical. I repudiate as clichéd and nonsensical the entire analogy, even in its more sophisticated manifestations, from whichever flank of the false and symbiotically-linked binarism it comes.

Numbers was very heterogeneous: we published many poets who would have gone smoothly into *Perfect Bound*. And I don't think poets should be assigned to particular ghettos because they happen to be published by one or other of the few presses that make poetry available in a relatively visible fashion. In short, I've thought, lived, and written my way out of an entire Joseph Cornell exhibition of conceptual boxes, and when not being attacked for failing to have the strength of my convictions (a familiar slur on the committed pluralist) I'm pretty happy with the situation.

I'd agree that the kinds of crude distinctions you mention are frustrating and misleading, though I've usually found that most of the writers I respect placed in the avant-garde camp are circumspect about making them — but let me end by asking: what do you think is the magazine's lasting achievement?

What counts in the longer run is what always did: is the material reread? If not, it's in perhaps permanent hibernation. No use lamenting that. All you can do is try to explain why certain things you like move you and deserve to be reread. There's an underlying optimism there, perhaps, that, with luck and creative help, the good will out and the fake will not hold people's attention for long. In this light, *Perfect Bound* will have done well if it contains even one or two poems per issue that are still read and talked about in another quarter of a century.

SIX

About their future

JANE DAVIES: *Can you tell us about what you think happens when you finish poems and they go out into the world — either at a reading or in published form? Do you ever think about their future? What happens when people receive them?*

Well, I do think about their future in the sense that I tend to write with a reader in mind, but it is a very unspecific reader. I sometimes write poems dedicated to people and I assume then that the dedicatees are going to be an ideal reader. But always there is the implication that the poem is going to be published and other people will hear it.

Is that reader an alter ego? A different corner of your self?

No, I don't think it can be, because obviously I read the poem; but I don't like the idea that I'm writing something that only I can understand or that only I can follow. That's bizarre. So this reader must be some kind of other — somebody else. I get reviewed now and then and sometimes reviewers come up with readings that are extraordinarily unlike what I had in mind. There's a poem in *Lost and Found* called 'Leaving Sapporo' about missing an aeroplane and about the Japanese professor who tried to drive me to the airport and who was very ashamed about the fact that we missed the plane. I wasn't that bothered about missing the plane; but I was bothered by his terrible feelings of anxiety. It was addressed to him. Recently there was this article in which the poem was linked up to all my earlier stuff, to things I'd written ten years before about sexual violence in Italy, and the idea of forgiving somebody turned out to be, according to this reader, that I was actually trying to forgive myself. Well, I swear I hadn't had that in mind, although I think the reading is perfectly plausible — and so I also have sometimes the feeling that readings come back at me and they're okay and they make sense. Sometimes they don't, but often they do. I don't think that my view of the poem's interpretability is the final word. I have that sense of a reader, too.

As it were something that's purely connected to the poem as a separate entity released into the world?

Then the poem becomes a sort of plant pot and some other flowers can grow out of it, which are not connected with me. And usually it's pleasant if this separate entity is something I vaguely recognise, but I don't at all think that's necessary.

I read some early poems with a class on Friday and people were very moved and disturbed by the poem that describes the incident of the rape . . .

'There Again'?

Yes. Could you talk about the construction of that poem? Because people were saying surely this can't have happened? How has he made it into a poem? As if the sense of trauma that is present in the poem —

They thought I'd made it up, in effect?

In the sense that it would have to be a report of something that had happened to someone you knew. Did you write it long after the event?

Five years, about. I didn't write anything at all for about four years and I think I didn't have any intention of writing anything about it, but what happened — I think I say this in the interview with Marcus Perryman, but I may be contradicting myself — I think what happened is that I started to find when I was writing about completely other things, or apparently other things, they seemed to be getting clogged up with hidden references to this background event and it seemed to me that there was something like a danger that I would start to write things that nobody would ever understand because there was this thing in the background — this thing forever pushing through into the poem but never being mentioned, and so I felt for two reasons (one to try to stop doing this thing of having seepage into the poems, and spoiling them or making them become rather odd) that I should confront it and deal with it, so that it would be there, present in my literary background . . . And I also began to feel that if I couldn't write about this, then how could I write about anything? That this was a something standing in the way of doing anything else.

Can you talk about what it's like being a poet and living in a foreign country? You spoke about that during the reading, phrases coming back . . .

English feeling fresh when you come back to England . . . I think the first thing to say is that when I went to Japan ten years ago I felt that my writing needed to change. I notice you've got a copy of

Entertaining Fates there. In that book, that book got criticized a bit, and the grammar in that book is very tortuous and in a way tortured and I was actually reading a lot of Browning at that time — thinking you could get away with it. Anyway, quite unintentionally I think going to Japan helped. I suddenly started to experience environments and so on which had very little reverberation for me, were rather flat, so I had to find the reverberations, and also I was teaching non-native speakers and as a result my spoken grammar and my written grammar had to be simplified. I started to give lectures completely without notes. In Cambridge, I used to read these complicated lectures out. In Japan I will just stand in front of the board with a photocopy and a piece of chalk and make it up as I go along, and so they can get me I say everything three times, of course, and I also say it in pretty simple declarative sentences. It's almost like the kind of process I might have deliberately set out to do if I were still in England, editing a poem down in some way for myself; that's partly what it's been like.

What about speech rhythms and things like that?

Well, I teach pronunciation too, to a language class of fourteen University bureaucrat recruits. I teach English speech rhythms and I do these very exaggerated versions of pitch, tone, intonational tune, weak forms, all that, and then get them to repeat them.

But has Japanese affected you?

No, I don't think so. I went there when I was thirty-five or six and I think it is too late. Its rhythms are so different. And it's a language that is nothing like English. I don't think it really interferes with English. I do know one or two people who speak no language at all — they speak English with Japanese phrases stuck in, ex-pats who've been there forever and who haven't really worried about the matter. My wife's Italian, so we have three languages going on in the house, because now my kids are learning Japanese at kindergarten. And we stick as firmly as we can to the rule that if you begin a sentence in one language you've got to stay with it to the end. *Finnegans Wake!* I'm living in it. Sean O'Brien in Tokyo said to me one time something like 'Don't you think that living abroad is impoverishing your vocabulary?' But it's not as if it were the nineteenth century or something. If I'd gone to Japan in the middle of the nineteenth century with no TV, no radio, no fax, no phone. . .

Possibly, but I think it must surely be like the business of Japanese not affecting you? The English is firmly in your head.

I'm being bombarded with American English, because it's the dominant one over there, so I'm quite capable now of saying to people, Americans for instance: 'Let's take the elevator'. I think it's enriched me. I would have thought my vocabulary has been enlarged.

So you have a relation to the iambic pentameter?

Do I have a relation to those very set English rhythms? Well, just recently I've started . . . I don't like the idea of writing in counted syllabics like Marianne Moore. Japanese poetry is written in syllabics (5-7-5 lines for a haiku, etc), and I started to become aware of the fact that if you wrote lines which have odd numbers of syllables then the lines tend not to fall into a too familiar English metre. The English metres tend to be tetrametric, octosyllabic tetrameters, or six syllable trimeters, or ten syllable pentameters . . . Even-numbered syllables. With two syllable feet. Roughly. So if you put an extra syllable onto the lines it's always going to give it a slightly ruffled feeling and then you can also use the syllable count to get another patterning going on. I only started doing that recently and at the same time not doing like Moore did, I think, where because you've got this syllable count you ignore metre and beat, or you think you can do almost anything. I personally think you can't; you've got to have the speech rhythms and the beat underneath it. I don't have a relation to the iambic pentameter, except that I feel uncomfortable with it. So I do have a complicated negative relation. But I like the ballad metre; I like the three-stressed line and then the four-stressed line, or vice-versa, and I like to have what you might call variable metres, so I love the English Pindaric ode: it's in metres but they are flexible and variable. That's where my sense of rhythms comes from.

I thought I could hear ballad rhythms when you were reading . . .

The three-quatrain 'Months Gone' is in ballad-form.

Is rhyme new?

There's more rhyme now than there was, but it comes and goes. As I've said before, I'm pretty eclectic about form. I don't much like the New Formalists in America because, it seems to me, they hit you over the head with the fact that it is always going to rhyme and it's always going to be in a set form. That seems to me rather polemically insistent in a useless way. It strangles the feel to the poem. So I don't like that kind of rhyming, but I have a sestina in *Lost and Found*, though I don't have any plans to write one again. I think there is more rhyme than there was, but it could go the other way.

Let me ask you about your notebook. The poems look to a stranger's eye as if you are writing them out pretty much whole.

But this one I read from is a fairly clean version; there are other drafts behind it which are just scribble.

How do poems come to you then?

There's no single answer to that. I write down little phrases, which then start to migrate from draft to draft. There's a page here that has just got little phrases on it, and some of them might get used and some might not.

Do phrases just come into your head?

That little bit in one of the new ones I read, this bit about '. . . its frost-crisped leaves / and others fossilized in asphalt' — I was looking around and there were leaves with frost on them. The phrase just came to me as I was walking along, and I wrote it down when I got back to the office. To save it for later. See if it fitted anywhere. Poems occasionally come in a great rush, but more often I'm like a magpie, and then something will click and the whole will come out.

You said you'd been writing one poem for a long time —

That was the one called 'Animal Sendai', the title's from *Finnegans Wake*, about the zoo. There's a draft of that from 1990, and I wrote it in 1998. And I wrote two poems about the zoo one after another, using those earlier versions as source material.

So how do you know when something isn't finished or isn't right?

Feel. That's the only thing I can say. I was reading an essay about Wittgenstein and Freud and Frazer by a professor of philosophy recently and he explained very clearly that what Wittgenstein seems to have been saying in those notes on aesthetics is that you can't have causal explanations for aesthetic effects. Frank Cioffi (who wrote the book) argues back that, in some carefully qualified way, you can. If somebody describes the sense of feeling uncomfortable in the face of a work of art, and you say 'Well, let me just change this bit and perhaps the discomfort will go away', I think the Wittgenstein idea is that you can't assume that there is some sort of simple trigger in the work of art that's producing the discomfort, whereas. . .

But do you mean that there may be complex triggers?

Well, I think there may be complex triggers, or there may be somethings that you can rationalize to yourself or explain to yourself. There can be explanations for aesthetic responses without the explanations having causal relations. I think the reason for that is that presumably a causal relationship would have to work every time. Whoever reads this poem at whatever time of day or night will feel this particular feeling — and this is obviously not how art works. So the question is what is it that is making you feel you've got to change something? And I would like to know more about what it is artists do feel, and whether they rightly or wrongly think that something in the work is causing it. I must do something more about this.

In the reader, then, when you are trying and failing to read, it's something to do with intensity of concentration, ability to create the object in your mind as you experience it, and when that's working well then it can be done. There may be other things, like your own emotional state and . . .

One thing is that you've got to be aware of the way that sometimes your own works are not going to work for you. So you mustn't tinker with things when you feel a bit flat.

That's a good rule.

You'll just destroy them. So one of the things is self-knowledge — now I'm in the right frame of mind to read this and to give it a go . . .

I find that really difficult. Do you just leave them for a long time?

I let them settle into themselves — to get away from your own projected feelings about them. To try to get the sense of what the thing is in itself, rather than what you want it to be.

What you think you're making?

And not to have too many over-determined rules about how you think it should come out. Allow the thing to go its own way. But I find with prose for example, with essays, I basically just give up. At a certain point you just feel I don't see what more I can do with this. But with a poem I don't think you do feel that, because I also hate that kind of plasticine feeling — you know, I can pull that head off, I can mush it around, I could do anything with it. I hate that feeling. I think that's connected with omnipotence, frankly. An unpleasant omnipotence.

That makes me think about the poem, 'All Around', about your acquaintance who committed suicide — where you asked wasn't this enough to have the trees, the day, to have a child . . . That when you are in a state of thinking I will stay alive and live my life it is on the basis of accepting that, however unsatisfactory your particular lot . . . but I don't know how I've got to this now from the poem.

Not straining for something that you can't have or have expectations of it that are way beyond anything you could ever live up to . . . My Dad said yesterday that nobody ever knows why somebody commits suicide, so I don't suppose I'll write a poem which explains it, or indeed whether that's really what I should be trying to do. I partly think, unfortunately, that this is one of those opportunities which has been thrown up where I've got a backlog of feeling about something and I'm sort of exploiting the occasion, I'm afraid.

Yes, it's partly that, but then that's what writers do all the time; it just feels worse when it is a large tragedy that is someone else's experience.

I just feel you have to be very careful and maybe not publish them too prominently or maybe . . . I get caught in the dilemma here . . .

It must have happened with the rape poems?

Well, people did wonder about that. Most of the reviews of that book, *This Other Life*, were good. But there was one review in *The Poetry Review* that said those poems were like me re-raping the girl — which I found absolutely horrific, and I mentioned this to my wife and she very kindly said: 'Don't worry about that one. You've done some bad things but not that.' But yes, it raises the spectre of that possibility, and certainly there are lots of debates about rape and representation, aren't there, which include that kind of thought. You grow up with the idea that writing is supposed to tell the truth and then you encounter all these checks on the truth, some of which are good ones, and so you've got to negotiate all that as well.

That's partly to do again with a personal thinking and a public voice. There are some things we don't say. But I don't think these poems are . . .

I'm rather alarmed by the possibility of being in the company of exploitative poems about rape, which do exist, some written by women too. Reviews have raised that spectre. That's part of the risk you have to run.

All your poems seem to address lived experience in recognizable forms of human expression — these big experiences have to be part of that.

You've put your finger on something that absolutely baffles me about the contemporary poetry scene. I thought this was what poetry did or does, and it often doesn't seem to, strangely enough, because most poetry now isn't much like this.

Why do you think that is?

Well, I am very puzzled by the way jokes are so important. In the '80s I helped organize a poetry festival in Cambridge, and the Italian poet Franco Fortini came, and he said to me: 'Why do all the English poems end with a little laugh?'

Well, people are very scared of being seen to be serious. You said yourself that you might be accused of being sentimental in that poem to your daughter?

So we've got this very hard skin on us that is quite false.

It's to do with private life not being a publicly reputable source of conversation. I think it's left over from the Seventies — from the time when it wasn't acceptable to have a private life. . .and it's not media sexy, being at home with the kids. So it was a relief to me to read somebody for whom the private. . . Do you have any followers, couldn't you found a school?

Not that I know of. No, I don't think so. I have a slightly saddened feeling about other poets — as if they, at some point or other, might have formed with me what I thought of as being a kind of group. Never with a slogan on it, just people who were about my age that were writing at the same time. Maybe it's the private life thing. The School of Private Life. But it didn't happen.

Tell me who has influenced you as a poet?

The problem with this kind of question is that I think my answer to it could go on all night. I can give you two straight off: one of them is Roy Fisher — who I came across at the age of 19 in Bradford University Social Sciences Library and I read those early poems of his about the demolition of Birmingham just like I was reading my own life. I thought this is what it's like, the mixture of social realism and weird, slightly paranoiac surreal twists . . . So in my early work there are strands of Roy Fisher everywhere. And I'm very glad recently, co-editing *The Thing About Roy Fisher* for Liverpool University Press, to have been able to honour this debt. I think I've managed to honour it. I hope so. Then there's an Italian poet that I came across about 1980: he's called Vittorio Sereni, and I translated him with a friend of mine in Italy. Sereni died in 1983, but I did just manage to meet him a couple of times before he died. His work is connected to Roy Fisher's through their both being influenced by William Carlos Williams. He was from Milan and Roy Fisher is from Birmingham: they both write out of these big, complex, but not capital cities. And I worked so hard on Sereni's poems that I could practically say then off by heart. Those two poets, without them I wouldn't be the kind of poet I am. But, interestingly enough, Fisher very rarely writes about his private life, and Sereni writes in a very guarded way about his.

You mentioned Browning before . . .

Browning, Hardy, Wordsworth . . . I studied John Donne at A level and I think those three complex stanzas — the *Songs and Sonnets* — they've got very firmly buried in me. Can't get away from Shakespeare, the Bible, I was brought up in the Church singing 'And did those feet . . .' and George Herbert . . .

You come from Bootle?

I was born in Salford. And then after a couple of curacies my father moved to St Andrews, Litherland, and I lived there from age 3 to 9, and then we had five years in Wigan. Then we moved to South Liverpool, Garston, in 1967. He was the Vicar of Garston until he retired. My parents now live just up the road in Mather Avenue. I went to Liverpool College; it had half-fees for the sons of the Clergy. I was in the same class as Simon Rattle . . .

Is there a reason you don't live in England?

I can't say that I'm an exile exactly. I couldn't get a job. I spent most of the '80s trying to get a job — coming second all the time . . . So I ended up doing endless, badly-paid freelance literature and language teaching around Cambridge. Finally, after about a decade of struggling, living on the credit card deficit, I got offered a visiting lectureship in Kyoto for a couple of years, talked it over with my wife, and she said: 'Why don't you go over to Japan and earn a bit of money.' It was just amazing suddenly to land up in this baffling place where I didn't have to work so desperately hard, and I used to take these very long hot baths, and for the first time in my life I relaxed about money, because of the regular salary. Then, in the second year, I was invited to take another job. It's just an annual job with a renewable contract, but I've been there for about eight years, and it seems to be going all right. I thought I was going for a break, but I've been there ten years. So I'm not an exile; I'm an economic émigré. That's why I'm abroad. I'd never in my wildest dreams have thought I'd live in Japan; I had no interest in the culture, didn't want to learn the language. I like it now — there are lots of good things about it. It's a very safe country, very well organized country, a very polite country. But it's where I work.

Have you always written poetry? When did you start?

I was about fifteen or sixteen. It all fits with an oedipal rebellion — one of the first things I ever wrote was a sort of rhyming essay for the RI teacher — rebelling against God and my Dad.

Are you still in rebellion?

No, I don't think so.

Do you have religious beliefs?

Well, I'm a religious sort of person, but I don't think I have the kinds of beliefs you could put into very orthodox positions or even unorthodox positions. I'm not a signed-up Zen Buddhist or anything, but I do think that having been brought up in religion it's very difficult not to have a religious turn of mind.

SEVEN

A tourist in your other country

PETER CARPENTER: *Many of your poems over the years have dealt with a sense of 'displacement' or being on the edge of things, not least due to the situation that you described in the note for* Anywhere You Like. *'I have grown more used to the idea that I'm now living in three different places: Japan, where I work; Italy, where my wife's family live; and England, where I was born. Of course, this is a state of mind, rather than a material fact.' Would you like to talk about the impact of this situation on your work, and the ways in which the textures of your poems evoke this as a 'state of mind'?*

Early printings of 'On Van Gogh's *La Crau*' have as an epigraph a few lines from Coleridge's poem to his brother George: 'Me from the spot where first I sprang to light / Too soon transplanted, ere my soul had fixed / Its first domestic loves . . .' That was putting a local habitation and a name to why I feel a sense of displacement practically all the time. I guess the impact of this situation on my work is just one of the founding facts about it. That's how I perceive the world. That's why there's something to report on — to Jean Kemp, for example, a little friend who I left behind when at the age of three I moved to Liverpool. So the state of mind is like Wordsworth in the Preface to *Lyrical Ballads* when he talks about the poet being peculiarly likely to be affected 'by absent things as if they were present' — to which I could add by present things as if they were absent. I might then be writing to register more forcefully to myself the presence of what is present, and to realize concretely the sensed presence of things absent, and then to accommodate both to each other. So I would imagine that the rhythms and the evocations and the occasioned speech in the poems are aiming at achieving some realization and integration of these disparate materials.

Would you talk a little about your methods of composition, the occasions of your poems? Have things changed at all over the years?

My first way of writing poems was to scribble down what I thought were cleverly turned bitter jokes that caught, or I imagined they did, the contradictions and injustices of the world as I became aware of them in early teenage. Then there was a phase of crude imitation in which I took a model like a Blake song, or a *Mauberley* quatrain poem, or a bit of Joyce's *Ulysses* and did an over-written version of it. The first poem I wrote which gets anywhere near my vein was about my father's dad, and was compared to a Beatles song by David Moody when I first went up to York in 1971. There I read in my first year Vladimir Mayakovsky's *How are Verses Made?* The *Waste Land* manuscript was published at about the same time. Then began a three or four year phase of imitating and absorbing and learning how to revise. Still, my only method was to slap down whatever came into my head and then slowly try to get some of the better bits to work as a poem. It was only in my mid to late twenties that I started learning how to listen for what was forming, put it down in a notebook, then slowly let it grow either in my head or on paper and, with luck and patience, both.

You seem to be quite prolific at the moment?

Yes, the poems have been coming unusually frequently over the last few years. Mind you, I've never ever worried about where the next one was coming from, and only very occasionally have I had droughts of a month or more. However, there have been times when the number of poems I thought publishable was suddenly very low. I used to have long bad patches. Perhaps I've got better at listening for the right things and letting them come naturally. Maybe the critical faculty is screening out wastes of effort before they even get started. Still, a prolific spell is just the time to grow wary.

What line, if any, do you take on the notion of a poem being 'abandoned' or 'completed'?

I don't abandon many poems, because I'm stubborn. When I've completed a poem I'll either decide it's not worth sending out, or send it out a few times, and then decide it's not right; or it will get accepted and then I'll wonder whether that means it's an acceptable poem or not. But I don't go along with the Valéry distinction at all. As far as I'm concerned 'abandoned' poems aren't finished and shouldn't be published. In other words, I don't make a fetish of perfection.

You have written about poetry and attempted 'reparation'. Would you like to talk about the relationship between this and revision?

I've done just that, at length, in my first critical book. There's an analogical relationship between 'revision' and 'reparation'. All of it goes back to the rape I witnessed when I was 'just a kid, maybe twenty-two, / Neither good nor bad, just a kid like you . . .' If you look at the poem 'There Again' it's all spelled out: writing the poem is seeing again what happened, and seeing again is 'revising', and in poetry 'revising' is, or we hope it is, making things better, and that might be, analogically as I say, performing an emblematic action in order to admit a measure of complicity, which is 'reparation', and so you write and revise in order to make things better. Well, it has to be attempted reparation, because the emblematic action in art can't be assumed to translate into life. The reader and the addressee have to take the measure of what the poem is doing. If they don't want to, there's nothing I can do about it: I'm on my own again. Barbara Everett caught this problem in a recent piece on the new J.C.C. Mays edition of Coleridge's poems when she wrote that the 'process of regret and redress can be carried out by a writer only as an act of communication, of sharing'. So I'm another forever trying to waylay wedding guests.

Then how do you feel about your reception over the years? Reviewers have found it hard to pigeonhole your work, but they still have a go (such as John Ashbery's re-working of Bloom's 'strong poets' in PN Review *to list you under the 'curiously strong'). Would you like to give them some guidance for future reference?*

T. S. Eliot says in his introduction to a choice of Kipling's verse that he's just trying to keep his man out of the wrong pigeonholes. I've taken that to heart and tried to keep out of all pigeonholes. Just to give a symptomatic instance of the problem from a recent, generous, and positive review for which I can't and shouldn't complain: there, the reviewer says I'm like Larkin and cites as evidence the single phrase: 'what will survive of us / is things'. But doesn't that mean that I'm veering away — note the pointed line break — from 'An Arundel Tomb' by the substituted noun, and signalling it by the odd grammar of the verb 'to be' with a singular subject and a plural predicate? The same poem ('Not Yet Out of the Wood'), being about an obsessive devotion to writing and how that is impacting on a relationship, is full of allusion to the poets. There's Dante in the title, Auden's Yeats elegy, W. S. Graham's analogy of snow and writing, a

Shakespearean stage direction, and a Giorgio Caproni epigram. The line that's supposed to be pure Larkin is crossed with a bit about his father's 'things' in Vittorio Sereni's 'Il Muro'. And the last line ('do I wait or go?') must be recalling Keats's 'Ode to a Nightingale'. Yes, I'm the sort of poet who likes poetry; and you don't need to 'get' these allusions to understand or enjoy the poem. But, then, if you're referring to allusions in a review? The kind reviewer also noticed that my *Selected Poems* contains an epigraph from Sereni's work and a dedication to him, and has probably noticed too that I've been involved in translations of his and other people's poems and prose. Yet there we are, I'm like Larkin, that poet who famously had no use for foreign poetry. So my advice to future reviewers would be just to try and do a good job: read it properly and then think about the cohesiveness of what you're saying about it.

Following on from this, many of your poems and essays show a heightened sensitivity regarding the reader or 'addressee' or 'interlocutor'. Would you talk about this, especially in your ability to turn, or change in pitch, modes of address within a poem, forcing the reader to re-appraise initial presumption?

How addicted we all are to talking about art with the vocabulary of bullying and torture! Am I 'forcing' anybody to do anything? The reader is entirely free to put the book down and not to 're-appraise' at all. If readers are doing that, then they are voluntarily undergoing the experience of allowing their minds and bodies to be moved by these words — which they themselves have to activate for anything to be happening. Sure, I like to put readers through their paces. One reason for this is that I'm the first reader, and in that sense I'm presumably the interlocutor being talked to as well. So I must be inviting myself to re-appraise my initial presumptions too. Another kind of answer to your question, though, would just be to go back to Jean Kemp and say that my poetry wants to talk to people I can't speak to any more: distant relatives, lost friends, people who've died. Or it wants to talk to those I can, my family, for instance — but to talk in ways that are not socially sanctioned, or which make something more emblematic of our words than the endlessly exciting and ephemeral stream of even the best conversation.

In a recent review of Christopher Reid's For and After in the TLS, you discussed the balancing act between private dedication and the public domain of readership: 'the danger in poems privately occasioned is that we can't merely be told of the significance in the event of life; we have to be allowed to live it once more with meaning.' Would you talk about the ways in which you deal with such a danger in your own writing?

By being very sparing with the dedications, for one thing. There are lots of 'unknown' interlocutors. Writing in a now-published private journal from 1989, Dylan Francis referred to my 'self-deprecating subject matter' as 'almost a stalking horse'. The thing is that I don't write about intimate relations of family, love, or friendship because, or only because, of their meaning in my life. After all, there are lots of people close to me to whom I have not dedicated poems, or rendered events of our lives into verse. How does the 'choice' get made? There has to be something that appears humanly and culturally worth exploring, evolving, developing, and perhaps resolving, in a piece of art. There has to be the light bulb going on in my head that says 'maybe there's a poem there'. So I deal with the danger (though I mentioned it in the review because it's been pointed to in poems of mine) by trying to write with the other interlocutors whom I don't know personally in the forefront of my mind. And the way to do that is to concentrate wholly upon what the words of the poem can be understood to mean by anyone who knows the English language and pays a reasonable amount of attention to those words.

Towards the end of your essay 'Envy, Gratitude and Translation', apropos Matthew Arnold's notion of the 'union of the translator with his original', you come to this conclusion: 'Translation is the correlation of significant differences.' Would you like to talk about your own experiences as translator in the light of this comment?

I made that comment in the light of my experiences as a translator and as a man loving a woman. I thought Arnold's remark sounded like fantasy sex. In a thoughtful review of the book of mine you published, *The Great Friend and Other Translated Poems*, the reviewer says that 'the skills of the translator, while restructuring the poem in its new language, lie in minimizing the losses'. Then he adds, quoting the blurb: 'if the aim becomes to make "English poems in their own right", something must give.' But I don't see why it must. There can be no union of the original with the translation. So they must be, at best, significantly different. The translator of poetry has to translate the fact that his text is a poem, and has to translate as closely as possible what it means, which, in the case of a poem also includes the occasion for its utterance and such like. I've been collaborating on translations of my own poems into Italian just recently. The texts will face each other. The aim has to be to have produced two poems. If the translation turns out well in its language, then I'm happy. If that requires rephrasing, or altering an idiom, or dropping the rhyme scheme, so be it. One of the things a faithful translator might do, after all, is to try and curb the desire to finesse an arbitrary gain, to out-do the occasion. That's what I meant by correlating the differences: you work on the translation so that it has its own integrity as English, and its integrity as a faithful approach to the original.

Changing tack only slightly, would you like to qualify or expand upon what a reviewer in the TLS called your 'important relationship with Vittorio Sereni'?

My wife is from Parma, where Vittorio Sereni's eldest daughter and literary executor lived. Those two poems, 'Unfaithful Translations' and 'Towards Levanto', bring together the work of translating Sereni and the process of falling in love, even though I was already married. So the important relationship is with my future second wife, and as far as Sereni is concerned the relationship is strictly with his poetry — which is being alluded to strongly in both those poems of mine. The close of 'Towards Levanto' ('the possible, Vittorio, your sea') links back to 'An Impossibility', dedicated to my now wife, and alludes to the third part of Sereni's 'Un posto di vacanza', which evokes feeling tempted by memories of sexual desire on that same coast. There are moves afoot to publish a large selection of Sereni's poetry and prose with an American university press, so perhaps making those links will become easier for people less familiar with European poetry. I only met Sereni himself twice before his painfully early death at 69. It would have been a pleasure, I think, to get to know him better; but it was not to be.

When did you start writing, and sending out for publication? Can you describe the motivations or promptings that started things off?

I started writing with an aim to make art at about the age of sixteen. Almost immediately I started giving things to people who were editing school publications. I submitted a sheaf of verses and won the 'Old Pupil's English Poem' prize at Liverpool College in June 1971. Then I appeared regularly in student magazines at York. I started sending out in about 1975. One of my earliest rejections was from Tim Longville at the *Grosseteste Review*. I had sent some would-be Objectivist lyrics — which I called 'Minimal Poems'. He wrote back a long and kind letter pointing out that they were nothing like 'minimal' enough to count. I hadn't read Cid Corman then. What was my motivation? One morning during my year in the lower sixth (we were studying *A Portrait of the Artist as a Young Man*) I woke up and just punched the pillow with the realization that James Joyce's book about his religion, sexual trouble, and Dublin made perfect sense of my religion, sexual trouble, and Liverpool. If he could do it, so would I. Doubtless, there have been thousands of young people who've had similar experiences; but, as I say, I'm stubborn and I stuck at it. I remember my A-level art master — he was also the Rugby coach — picking up one of my expressionistic landscapes about then and saying: 'Rob, Rob, what are you trying to prove?' Good question.

Would you talk a little about editorial policies and your decisions in placing poems with particular poetry magazines and journals? Your poems are to be found in 'shoestring' avant-garde journals such as Shearsman *or* Tears in the Fence, *and well-heeled places like the* TLS . . .

My answer would have to be prefaced by the fact that decisions made about where my poems appear have not tended to be made by me! I have a drawer of rejection slips I occasionally open and immediately close again. One of the consequences of trying to keep out of the pigeon holes may be that you don't feel perfectly at home in any magazine. They are all slightly disorientating galleries in which to find things on display. The oddity of my appearing in the very precarious ones and in a News International paper on alternate weeks, as it were, is the result of suddenly being 'taken up' by a few of the main venues at the age of 50. I fear that their interest may well prove a flash in the frying pan. Someone said recently he'd seen another of mine in the *TLS*; and then added that I had clearly perfected the art of the one-inch-deep poem. You're just not likely to see a three-page piece of mine, 'The Relapses' for instance, in that paper. No, it appeared in John Matthias's *Notre Dame Review*, the nearest thing I have to a home in the USA. The shoestring magazines are the places where I started publishing; and the ones I like have friendly editors with distinctive, but still pretty catholic tastes. There are some poets I hear who only allow their work to appear in 'the best' places. I wouldn't like to have that sort of attitude. If practically anybody asks me for something, I tend to send. Living a long way from everywhere, I find it reassuring to keep up contacts with a wide range of publications. Not being able to draw sustenance from the ground any longer, I'm the kind of plant that has had to develop a large number of air roots.

Could you talk a little about Perfect Bound *and* Numbers, *two magazines that you helped to edit . . .*

One of the first galleries where I thought my work hung rather oddly was *Perfect Bound*. 'Worlds Apart', in the first issue and the first poem in the *Selected Poems*, sounds too personal, provincial, and human — all too human, for that particular zoo. The various issues of the magazine might be seen as an attempt to surround my poems with work that would make it appear less lonely, or simultaneously with attempts to write in ways that would not stick out so much — both impossible, more or less, in the end. We had a rule with *Numbers* that the two editors who were poets wouldn't publish their own work (though we allowed translations). *Numbers* was a bit like that definition of a camel: a horse designed by a committee. We produced some interestingly varied issues; but it was instructive to find that we would endlessly debate whether to publish a couple of poems by an obscure figure from one clique or another, while the big names from those same cliques would get in on the nod. That was upsetting.

Have there been any defining moments in your career to date, what reviewers like to call 'breakthrough moments'?

I don't think of myself as having a career as a poet or a writer. For me it's more of an obsession. People go into a career with the idea that it's going to give them a salary. Speaking in those terms, though, a breakthrough moment might be when John Welch of The Many Press agreed to do a collection with a spine in 1979. It might be when Michael Schmidt at Carcanet said he would look at a manuscript in 1985 and eventually accepted it. Then there's the day Martin Dodsworth reviewed that book — *This Other Life* — in *The Guardian* (13 May 1988), a day I walked around in a daze of fondly imagined fulfillment. Or there's the evening he gave the book a little prize in that same year. I've been lucky. There have been lots of them. But in terms of the obsession, well, it's moments like one night and morning in September 1976. I went to bed in Little Venice after just noting down straight the first seven lines of 'Overdrawn Account' as they stand in the *Selected Poems*, and then woke up with the following twenty-one waiting to be written. That was one of the first poems that 'just came out that way' and I liked it.

How difficult was it to 'select' for your Selected? *Was it especially difficult to choose from the early work?*

Not very — I just picked the ones that demanded not to be left out. The early work was the easiest, because there are poems there that strike me as tentative steps down roads not really taken. They can, most of them, go into a *Collected Poems*, all being well, but those pieces complicate the early story with hesitations and I thought they could be spared the dim glare of further publication for now. There were also early poems, 'Some Hope' for instance, where I had wanted to print a revised text almost from the moment that they appeared in the first pamphlets and collection.

Over the years, since we first met in 1979, what, in the words of your 1997 collection's title, have you 'lost and found'?

Ah yes, 'The art of losing isn't hard to master', as Elizabeth Bishop has it. I've lost my first love, and our precariously settled situation in Britain. We were finally divorced in about 1994. I've lost the hearing in one ear, from the very invasive surgery required to remove a brain tumour in 1993. I've lost the ability to cry out of my right eye and my broad and balanced smile, for the same reason. I've lost the feeling, or merely assumption, that my native land is where I ought to be. I've lost illusions about the literary world and the literary life — but perhaps not all of them. I've gained my second love, whom I first met in 1984 and married eleven years later. I've been able to have a family: two daughters. Thanks to the Japanese education system, I have a job and a salary. Thanks to many people, including you, I've a reputation, or something like the start of one, for what I am able write.

EIGHT

A sense of process

KATY PRICE: *My first question is about how your poems are ordered within a collection or sequence. There is a sense of process at work in each of your books so that the disposition of a single poem is often modified by what has gone before and what follows it. Do you rearrange your poems once the bulk of a new collection has formed, or are they simply given in the order that you wrote them?*

I got this sense of a book from Baudelaire's *Fleurs du Mal* and had it reinforced when encountering Vittorio Sereni's four volumes. In my case, it depends on which pieces or collections we're talking about. There are sequences like 'The Benefit Forms' where there is a skeletal narrative going on. The poems were written and heavily revised in the order that they came to me over about three years. They were sequenced and worked together during that time into the set of ten, plus 'Some Hope' as a kind of coda. The poems about a rape in *This Other Life* are, really, a sequence but they were written even more separately as single efforts then sequenced so as to attempt a therapeutic shape.

There are basically two possible sequencing principles throughout: one is the order the poems were composed, the other the temporal sequence of events or occasions explored. The books which come closest to combining these are *Lost and Found* and *About Time Too*. The first is all but a poetic diary of occasions from May 1989 to September 1993. The latter has the poems sequenced in something approaching the order that they were written between December 1993 and late summer 1998.

The first three books represent an intermittent precipitate of the best I could do at the time, work often collaged from vast heaps of draft pieces. *This Other Life* contains poems put together over ten years, and the sequencing came slowly between 1978 and 1988. More recently, I've started to let the poems sequence themselves as they come out, doing no more than dropping the ones that don't convince me — or magazine editors repeatedly — as I'm working and sending them off. Also, I'm not living the kind of eventful life just now, thank goodness, that would ask to be made into a diaristic narrative.

How have you gone about choosing poems for the Selected, *and have you found any new or unexpected relations forming between the poems?*

I've chosen the ones I like best, or ones that seem to work best, or things characteristic of what I do: the ones people mention in reviews, that sort of thing. . . and I've also put in early ones that I like, but have wanted to publish in revised forms for a long time. Most of the revisions you might notice to earlier poems were done years ago. I recall reading the three-part version of 'Some Hope', for instance, in the early 1980s. One lucky, unsuspected relation that I've played up is that by ending the *Entertaining Fates* section with 'On Van Gogh's *La Crau*' then beginning the *Lost and Found* one with 'An Undetermined Heart' I've pulled out a thread about my unsettled vicarage childhood. More often, though, I'm conscious of the pieces missing between the chosen landmarks. Early on, there's some attempt to get the chronologies of occasions and dates of composition to match better. Later, I've just reprinted from the books, but with poems missing. In the last section, I've selected in the same fashion from a draft collection that is now more or less completed, but not yet ready to publish entire.

In Poetry, Poets, Readers *you explore the ability of poetry to make things happen, and this means getting away from the idea of a separate world inhabited by poetry. You follow Wittgenstein, writing that in poetry 'the unutterable will be — unutterably — contained in what has been uttered'. So poetry brings out the 'unutterable' in life — but aren't unutterables necessarily elusive of formulae or methods for capturing them?*

Back in my undergraduate days I became aware of Mallarmé's remark about mentioning a flower and losing the perfume — the idea that if you name something directly you may short-circuit its poetic charge. And I recall in student workshops harping on about the bit of a would-be poem that should be cut because it was the part in which the writer told instead of showing. This sounds like some of the cultural baggage out of which Wittgenstein's own remark about unutterables may have come.

I take your point about how you can't have a formula for the 'unutterable'. That's quite a good test of a poem, because a formulaic 'mystery' is a put-on. The poem will be a tease. The reader is being abused. So the unutterable has to be substantially on the edge of what the poem can be brought to utter.

Has your approach to unutterables changed over the years?

Going over the proofs recently, I notice that 'Faith in the City' has 'the unspeakable' in it, and then 'There Again', the next poem from *This Other Life*, has 'the unutterable'. Back in the early 1980s, what couldn't be said in relation to my family background, and in relation to the rape, were quite enough to be going on with. Those matters have probably now been made as utterable as they're going to be, but life is literally full of unutterables: you just catch someone gazing abstractedly at something and their slightly wistful face seems to be written all over with meanings that are never going to be said, that the person might never be in a position to articulate. Art might be waiting in the wings right there.

The idea of a face written over with unsayable meanings suggests an analogy between poetry and painting; your poems might be read as realist paintings that enliven the presented faces of the world. Obviously the canvas of a poem is rather different to that of a painting, but do you work consciously with aspects such as depth and surface, for example?

James Lasdun was spot-on when, reviewing my first book over 20 years ago now, he said I seemed a painter *manqué*. The things in the first section of the *Selected Poems* were done at a time when I was also painting a lot, and even exhibiting a little. I still do the occasional picture when the mood takes me. Textures, surfaces, perspectives, points of view, figures and grounds, light and shadow — they all come into it, but, as you say, the space of a poem seems quite a different proposition to that if a picture — even if I did a bit of exploring in the areas of Cubist poetry when starting out.

Is the term 'realism' relevant to you as a poet?

I can't escape it. Even a poem like 'Out of Circulation' — which is one of the very few I've written that attempts to report a dream — turned out like a bit of northern realism with some mysterious goings on in it. My understanding of the term, though, comes out of studying Roy Fisher when young. I read around in Russian Formalism and got the point that it's a type of making-strange too. Is Lowry a realist or an expressionist? Because poems don't have to produce an overall scannable picture, but a linear selection of significant details, they can be vastly distortive for expressive purposes, yet still give off an 'air' of being just descriptions of how things were: 'The Happiness Plant', for example. Poems are intensively expressive — like a person's hands and face, after all.

Your own poems use observation of the physical environment successfully time and again, but there is restlessness about the business of observation. As a reader I don't find myself thinking 'here goes Peter Robinson, gazing at trees again'. Has there been a conscious development to your art of observation?

I'm glad you don't have that thought about me and trees. Perhaps you don't because I sometimes do? But to work back from the specific question, I'm not aware of a conscious development in observation and describing. What may have happened behind my back, as it were, is that as you get older you get to know your way around your own mind better and while early poems described effects of daylight or wind in grasses, or brick and stone, because these were charged with a sense of meaning that I couldn't have put a finger on, and so described to find out what it was, as you keep returning to these things, and try not to repeat yourself too, then you become more conscious of thematic content expressed by the descriptions. So they can become more laconic and yet more pointed.

One striking example of this development is along the theme of cracks. I'm thinking of the ending of 'Some Hope', where 'Some hope cleaves as moss and grass / cling to a sheer face, cracking the stone / to flakes of raucous laughter, / an access for some eye to work'. In subsequent collections the cracks reappear in increasingly laconic forms; for instance the crumbling walls and cracked paving slabs of '472 Claremont Road', or even more subtly in the recurrence of frozen or derelict scenes. Elsewhere you have identified the frosted glass of '472 Claremont Road' with the disposition of your poems, which 'half reveal and half conceal their occasions' (in the Oxford Poetry interview with Ian Sansom). Do these cracked stones also have a story to tell about poetry?

I'm fond of old brick walls where the pointing has gone and the mortar is crumbling away. Putting sentences together is usually better when it has the feel of a dry stonewall being built, rather than papering over the cracks in the plaster. I realize too I have Tennyson to thank for that phrase about frosted glass . . . So I must have been talking about grief that won't go away, grief that is only partially assuaged by poetry.

There's a recent and conscious revisiting of the 'cracks' theme in 'By the Way': 'while from each fissure / push the flowering dandelions'. There's quite a lot of nature reclaiming her own in poems of mine — and from the beginning too.

Do you have to work at balancing writing about the processes of poetry with the things that demand to have poems written about them? Is there any such distinction in practice?

There's a fine line to walk here: if you don't know what you are doing, your poems about things that need to be written about will be almost certainly bad. Then again, if you only know what you are doing, the poem will be *'voulu'* and bad again. If poems are just one only-too-obvious 'Thought Fox' after another, then they're bad. If they crack along utterly oblivious of the fact that they are poems, they're bad in yet another way. Ideally, there may be no distinction between the way a good poem is about something and simultaneously about itself being about something. In practice, there are innumerable ways for the two attentions to fail perfectly to coincide.

You say your poetry has grown 'more laconic and more pointed' as you've got to know your own mind better and become more conscious of thematic content. Are there other ways in which you feel your poetry has consolidated earlier concerns?

No, I'm not conscious of any such consolidations, except in so far as the barely sketched tensions and anxieties of the early work were fleshed out in the second book, and then, perhaps, followed up in more wide-ranging and generic terms through later ones. What I am rather conscious of is that if you were to take the portrait of my paternal grandfather in 'World's Apart', the first collected poem, as inevitably containing self-portraiture, then I'm really not sure to what extent I have avoided his pitfalls, not sure to what extent the poems that follow show us as so very different.

Are there ways in which you're now aiming to develop your style, or are such things best managed tangentially?

I'm a great believer in not predetermining directions and developments, in thinking about 'my themes' as little as possible — as you say, letting that happen tangentially. But I have thought to myself that I would like to be able to write successful poems that were either shorter or longer than the ones I usually do. I'm not asking for much: just the capacity to do an epigram, and a poem that turns the page four or five times. Aside from such simple notions of developing my range, I try to read against the grain of my temperament. I try to make a point of reading poets that 'I'm not supposed to like'.

Can you give some examples of poets that you weren't supposed to like, and what you have gained for your own work from reading them?

What I meant by 'not supposed to like' was something on the lines of — writers other than those reviewers would mention in the same breath as me, or the sorts of writers that I privately find, or found at first, hard to take. Whitman is someone I just couldn't get on with for years. Then, starting in the late 80s, I set myself to try and appreciate him. The anaphora in the last verse of 'Leaving Sapporo' was done with his methods of going-on in mind. Borges's poetry would be another. A recent poem 'Against Himself' (*TLS*, February 2002), based on a double-exposure photo of my uncle defeating, or losing to, his other side at chess, was helped along by Borges. One way to put this more generally might be to say that I've a distinct sensibility with a tendency to find value in certain ways of doing things — and to use a repertoire of methods for both upset and reassurance. An early and perpetual favourite is Hardy. But there's a world of other cultures, lives, subjects, ways of doing things, and I've done my best to work against the potential restrictions of that 'given' sensibility and temperament. That's one reason why I like quite a lot of Italian poetry: its expressive registers are so different. My assumption must be that since I am definitively something and will never escape it, that leaves me free to feed it with all sorts of distinctly other materials to see what it can digest and in what ways it can evolve.

So you really have been trying to avoid the pitfalls of 'World's Apart', because unlike your paternal grandfather whose own 'world suffices' you are always looking outside?

My grandad's case is sadder than that early poem makes out. When I wrote it, I put 'but something caused his / rush home to her' and that's as much as I knew. More recently one of my brothers told me he returned to Manchester at some point between the wars to apply for nationality so as to emigrate to Canada, but was turned down on health grounds. He never quite got over the setback, apparently. This is one of the things that has made me an English poet. Now I'm not sure that his world did suffice; it's more likely he didn't have a choice. So there's the self-portraiture in my account of him: what I describe as his fate is the one I'm afraid I'll re-enact — hence perhaps, as you say, my efforts to read poetry in foreign languages, to live in different cultures, to be in dialogue with others.

You said earlier that your life now is not as 'eventful' as it may have been in the past, but even in the early poems there is a sense of event about the most mundane of things. A favourite of mine is 'Pressure Cooker Noise' from the Rosemary Laxton *sequence. There is a grim humour that seems to thrive on conditions inside the rather claustrophobic flat, and the form of these poems feels as though it is coming to life through adversities encountered there. The gappy lineation of 'Pressure Cooker Noise' is not gratuitous; it strikes me as integral to maintaining a sense of self in that pressurized atmosphere. So does your poetry require adversity in order to develop?*

'Pressure Cooker Noise' was written in 1977, I think, about two years after the rape had happened. All those early domestic poems are shadowed with it, but unable even to touch on it.

I hadn't realized about the dates, because A Part of Rosemary Laxton *was published several years before the sequence about the rape in* This Other Life. *It gives the pressure a much more distressed inflection, and suggests that those poems had no choice about the unutterable facing them. So that particular source of adversity must have stayed with you, and with your poetry, indefinitely.*

If you've got damage and difficult experiences that go back very early — and I'd already felt the urge to write long before the more dramatic events in the earlier poems happened — then you may have reservoirs of adversity that are still there in need of fitting emblems even when the outward course of life seems to be running fairly smoothly.

And have the uses of adversity shifted since those early days?

Most probably. When you're working to get the poems to succeed in any way or shape or form, adversity can drive you on, but you may not be able to do much with it in the work itself. Later, that kind of bare success in producing something may not seem enough. It's possible that as you develop the quality of poems that get put aside for revision, or forever, goes up. I am glad you like the lineation of

'Pressure Cooker Noise', and the idea that lineation is responding to pressure is another way of saying that form is thematic meaning, which I believe. It struck me recently that a general term for what produces an occasion for a poem with me might be 'ambivalence' — and there seems to be no shortage of that around, even if there's more calm and happiness too.

Could you say a bit more about the ways in which ambivalence helps to produce the occasion for a poem? Perhaps there are particular poems or occasions that have required the cultivation of ambivalence to see them through?

What prompted this thought were my feelings as I repeatedly arrive in and leave Italy, England, or Japan — the feelings I have as I get on a fast train or an aeroplane. 'Perpetual Elsewhere' identifies the ambivalence of not wanting to stay and not wanting, though finally having, to leave. Then the recent longer piece, 'The Relapses', which is set in England, Liverpool in fact, contains the phrase 'balancing a choice of nostalgias' — about the uneasy sense of always hankering to be in one of my other countries.

Are there times when ambivalence needs to be resisted, resolved or thrown off?

I'm ambivalent about that ambivalence too. Having various conflictual feelings about the culture wherever I happen to be seems only realistic, but never feeling wholly committed to anywhere I am is not so positive. Poems are going to be occasioned and motivated by such feelings, but they aren't likely to be resolved with them.

So does ambivalence have limits that can usefully be tested through poetry?

As I say, the poems themselves are two-faced about ambivalence: they like it because this gives them material and energy, as well as thematic complexity, but they don't like it because you could get trapped in that kind of chaos and never get out. The endings of many of my pieces have the air, to me at least, of a holding operation. They don't necessarily resolve the conflicts or solve the problems, but they do perhaps find a way of balancing the claims of the ambivalences, of expressing the different pressures. The end of the poem is then a bit like a dramatic 'curtain line' at the close of the second act of a three act play. It says 'go and have some refreshment, then please came back for more.' So, yes, poems can benefit from, partly by testing, those limits.

I'd like to return to your comment about form as thematic meaning. There is a watchful nonchalance about your forms that I find very appealing; the poems act as though they are always rediscovering, rather than working to cultivate, their poise. Can you talk about some of the ways in which you have worked with form?

In the very early poems I'm experimenting with different lengths of line, trying to shift very quickly from the short to the long; but I've never liked the sound of 'arbitrary' or 'imposed' form, so there had to be something natural-sounding about the transitions. It struck me in my early 20s that you could find infinite variations if you just took all the standard metrical forms from the two- to the seven-stress line and worked out how to use them with one, two, or occasionally three weaker stresses between the strong ones. I got the idea first instinctively and then more professionally that there aren't just two types of stress, weak and strong, but — as on a sliding volume control — an innumerable number of positions depending on the relative weights of the syllables placed next to each other. I've made a point in the past of learning how to use stressed syllables placed together, and I experimented with the one-stress line of two or three syllables too.

That was the apprenticeship, and since then I've gone through phases of being more or less conscious of the number of syllables in the line, the number of lines in a stanza, and so on and so forth. I've also moved back and forth between the degrees of casualness I'm comfortable with, the amount of rhyme that's going on, such-like things. I've tried to keep right away from any dogmatic positions on metre, formalism, free verse, or any of the other corners you can paint yourself into. That leaves the kinds of structures I feel comfortable with, or which my sorts of poem seem to find for themselves, plus the attention to habits, bad habits, and the need to keep fresh, and not get into ruts.

So how does a form take on meanings?

As an undergraduate, I wrote a dissertation on the political allegiances of vers-libre in Rimbaud and Laforgue. I can't remember what conclusions I came to, but it was likely the start of scepticism about any fixed analogies between types of form and the ideas or feelings about cultures, politics, other people, that they may represent or express. Nowadays, I believe that poems themselves thematize the formal devices that shape them. After all, a caesura or an enjambment or a stanza-break are literally nothing. They are silence; they are white space. However, the words we use for them — a cut, a leap, a room-divide, are already all metaphorical. A silence can be made to signify almost anything, depending on what's around it. The sensitivity of the reader — and the writer is only a reader who has the right to make changes — is where the possibilities for meaningful relationships between the language and the language-as-shaped are born.

I like to be surprised by my own poems, so have never understood what benefit there would be in writing as a form of achieved and repeatedly demonstrated mastery. Each poem is a new set of occasions for the solving of innumerable technical problems (all poems are experimental poems, as Wallace Stevens says), and I go along with T. S. Eliot when he said that there is no saying where technique begins or ends . . . After all, when it comes to the overall result of a new poem, the writer is in a similar position to the reader. I have to find out what it amounts to as well.

You've said elsewhere (in the Poetry Kit *interview) that during your undergraduate years you wrote a lot of poetry imitating various styles.*

One of the things I did start to get by experimenting as a student was the beginnings of a feel for what sounded right and what didn't, as well as taking some first steps in learning what readers might have an interest in and what they wouldn't. I was recently sent a set of twelve untitled poems that I gave to a school friend in early 1975. Two or three of them I had copies of because they'd been published in magazines, but the others were lost. It was interesting to see how phrases and the germs of phrases were taken up almost unchanged in later work, or were developed into poems written over a decade later — '472 Claremont Road', for instance. So these twelve poems, plus a very different earlier version of what became 'The Benefit Forms' (which I've also lost), represent my work when a step or two away from being fledged.

Looking back, what do you think distinguishes the poems in Part One of the Selected *from those early exercises?*

There are various differences: little sense of a poem's design, gestures which are either inert or over-expressionistic, precious little undercurrent of wit, crudely ironical reverses, cadences that are not quite timed properly, rhymes that are a little too heavy. . . I could go on. Those twelve poems are written in a rather prissy short-lined form, an attempt at the lightly structured neo-objectivist lyric. But it didn't deliver enough for me. I needed a dose of Ed Dorn's earlier outspokenness in 'On the Debt my Mother Owed to Sears Roebuck', or 'From Gloucester Out', or 'An Idle Visitation' to approach the sense of something having been unburdened in 'World's Apart' (as well, of course, as Charles Tomlinson's 'John Maydew *or* The Allotment' to diverge from); and I needed an obsessive reading of Pierre Reverdy's cadences to get 'How He Changes'. They're the earliest surviving works to be republished.

In Poetry, Poets, Readers *you talk about Abraham Cowley locating promises in his early poems that he felt his later works did not quite fulfil. 'Some Hope' strikes me as a promissory poem, because it explicitly rewrites the 'salmoning cloud' and 'township's stone' of the tenth 'Benefit Form', and prefigures key themes and images of subsequent collections. It's interesting to see that in the* Selected *the relationship between the main sequence and its coda has shifted, with the omission of five 'Benefit Forms' and the addition of a new middle section to 'Some Hope'.*

Actually, I finished the first part of 'Some Hope' first and then lost confidence in it, so reused some phrases in a final draft of the last 'Benefit Form'. In the meantime, I had given a sheaf of poems to my supervisor, and he picked out 'Some Hope' as one of the better ones. It was sent off to *Palantir* and accepted on a first outing, appearing in June 1977. There were three poems by Roy Fisher in the same issue. We had met at the Cambridge Poetry Festival that April, and he wrote complimenting me on it — as well as noting my indebtedness to him! A happy moment.

But it left me with a dilemma about the last part of 'The Benefit Forms'. About this time I discovered that Mandelstam had reused phrases in different poems and I thought, well, why not? If I put 'Some Hope' immediately after that sequence, then you would read from 'then this voice came through' to an echo of the poem's lines in more distended cadences. It can slightly wrong-foot people, but I like it. As I say, the middle part of 'Some Hope' was written at the same time as the rest, in 1976, but I didn't think I'd got it right. It does at least give a hint of why the young people are leaving the North — and having published this version I feel I've finally fulfilled my part of the bargain towards that poem. I've given the five 'Benefit Forms' with their original part numbers to indicate that this short version is just for the *Selected Poems*. It's not a revision, just a selection for this occasion only.

Do you read any promises in those early poems, and has your later work been able to keep them?

Isn't that something only a reader can decide? I would prefer to keep my options open on that question, and just continue trying to fulfil them. After all, I might be only halfway round the course and, as in that sentence from Roy Fisher's 'Releases': 'It's amazing what you can say if you try.' With sequences like 'A Burning Head' or 'Scargill House' I felt that something was taking shape that would have been quite beyond me when starting out — not to mention the poems about the Italian rape only begun five years after it had happened — and the entire slice of my work that relates to Japan was not even dreamed of in, never mind promised by, those tentative settings out.

Many of the adjustments made to your earlier poems clarify perspective, yet a vital shifting of outlook is retained. This inability to produce a stable interpretation is a strong weakness, providing Lost and Found *with its opening 'A Dedication' in which you 'say / words of explanation and launch them on the air.' When poems are launched on the air do they defy the biographical conditions that produce them?*

Perhaps 'defy' is the word for it — as if I were trying to keep the poem and the circumstances together, but, like quarrelling siblings, they are always standing off and defying each other. Well, I not only like works of art that come trailing clouds of context, but I believe that the occasions and conditions in which a work of art is produced stick and remain as embedded aspects of it even as it sets off on its time travelling. So I don't go along with the only too familiar notion that a work of literature has 'history then, and timelessness ever after'. It has history as long as it lasts.

The departure point of a poem may well be autobiographical, but the arrival can't be. It may look as if some lyric poets are obsessed with their own lives, but that can be deceptive. If you put a first-person singular pronoun into a poem, it may well be making space for other people. If you leave it out, the entire text, whatever it appears to be about, will likely be an unmitigated self-projection. The prudence of people in relation to their interests is quite likely to preclude the kinds of interest that writers might be able to take in their lives for the purposes of making art. After all, you have to turn the uniquely specific into the emblematic, or representative. You have to reveal the possible meanings in the occasion, and not just stop at a meaning that flatters you yourself or anyone else.

If you put a 'you' into a poem, it's always going to suggest a possible 'talking to myself', an address to a real and familiar or imagined intimate interlocutor, and then an address to the reader too. Just to negotiate these three possibilities, and try and appreciate those three potential needs in the behaviour of the text, is to locate the work in a space for meanings some way off from the explanatory in any merely self-justificatory sense.

The humour in your poetry often arises from disturbance of some kind, for instance a man 'trying to smooth / lumps from packet soup', or, later on, your daughter crying in a consul's office. And there's a characteristic shrug of humour in certain titles — 'Some Hope', 'An Undetermined Heart', About Time Too. *Do the smiles in your poetry simply break out of their own accord, or do they need to be coaxed?*

I was lying in the bath in 1997 when the phrase 'Marking Time' impressed itself on me as also marking the vectors for a possible poem. It was the week of the year when we mark thousands of entrance exam scripts; it was a moment when, because of that duty, I couldn't return to Europe where my wife had recently given birth to our second daughter, so I was marching on the spot and not going anywhere; and, waiting to be teased out in the composition of the poem, there was the matter of how, more variously, time is marked in life, or how time marks life — by seasonal change, by hopes and expectations, by disappointments. . . So, sometimes, the smiles just break out and practically write the poem of their own accord. At other times they are added after the writing to establish an air of equivocation in the situation of the poem. I think that's how it was with 'Some Hope'. Sometimes they need to be coaxed: *This Other Life* was called *From the Life*, the name of a poem which had to be left out at the last minute, and *About Time Too* was first *The Colouring of the Past* (a theme retained in the book's epigraph), then merely *About*

Time — which, now I think of it, has a similar colloquial flavour, but also an over-ripe tang of the philosophical treatise about it . . .

Do some jokes have to be held back?

The early poem now called 'Tokens of Affection', a phrase lifted from the poem itself, used to have an elaborately punning title on the 'La donna è mobile' theme. But there was a trap for the unwary young poet in the phrase 'the furniture is bolted down' which also means, irrelevantly, 'eaten in a hurry'. It had to go, and it might well have been held back by a more mature writer.

In your writing about poetry as well as in your poems there's a syncretic style, a need to incorporate opposing principles without a compromise. Poems both pretend and are serious; differing views of a physical or emotional landscape are incorporated into a working whole. Do you find philosophy a help when it comes to managing these differences — as a critic and as a poet?

'The Gift' makes an allusion to Dr Johnson's remark when asked why he was stuffing orange peel into his pocket. To a poet anything may turn out to be useful, and that includes philosophy. The sources for inclinations in the directions you mention may well have started out from Jesus's various remarks and silences about neighbours, enemies, and women taken in adultery — which I have from my vicarage childhood. Then they will have been helped along by Keats on fixities and definites, Empson on surviving amid contradictions, Adrian Stokes writing about aesthetic and psychological integration. Though I read some individual works of philosophy in my graduate student years, it was only in my 30s that I began to read philosophy in any sustained way. So Bernard Williams's essay 'Moral Luck' or Arthur Danto on ready-mades and Pop art were feeding tendencies already formed. The Williams essay was helpful in drawing attention to the fact that in practice you can't settle moral and cultural conflicts by cost-benefit calculations, but you equally can't allow certain individual resistances to block necessary change. That sort of problem sponsors thought along the lines of how incompatible positions can be brought to live together coherently. But with reading philosophy it's obviously not possible to say in advance whether a particular book will help or hinder. I get much more from *Human, All Too Human* than I do from *Zarathustra*, for instance. All in all, though, I'm plumping for 'a help'.

Can poetry also be a help when philosophy hits a wall? Philosophy often entails confronting apparent opposites, and in practice it can be difficult to believe both. A rational argument is required and there are limits to how far rationality can be manipulated before one ceases to be philosophical and starts being mystical, or impossible. Do you find poetry a help here, perhaps as a rogue branch of philosophy in which the rules of rationality can be played with?

No, I don't think of poetry as a rogue branch of philosophy, and can't really see the gain in doing that. Maybe this can be approached the other way round. There are occasions in life where it feels necessary to live by strictly contradictory views of what to do — not only feels necessary, but it's something we have to do in order to get through a tricky phase, or manage a difficult person, or balance the claims of friendship with those of family, spouse with parents, or whatever it might be. A rational or logical approach to the problem may produce a strictly correct course of action, but not the most humanly responsive and, therefore, most beneficial one. Here a long exposure to the multiple and simultaneous perspectives of poetry might just stand you in better stead than the drive to a strictly coherent, defensible position.

At the reading end, this kind of difference in approach may show in the examples philosophers use which, even when they are attempting to confront a complex decision, often feel like fleshless skeletons. Bernard Williams concedes this for his Gauguin case in 'Moral Luck'. He trims off the messy detail in order to concentrate on the philosophically illuminating 'dilemma'. Poetry is perhaps more helpfully exercised by just that messy detail.

In your more recent poems there is a bolder sense of what the words can and can't do, and a sharper equivocation about images embodying or slipping away from experience. I'm thinking for example of the clouds 'whose nuances / shape themselves' in 'Farther Adventures', or the railway weeds in 'Listen to the Summer'. There are stronger regularities and repetitions, too, as if the lines are girding themselves for something. Is this a new 'phase of inspiration', the result of some impatience?

I'm just trying to see how far the styles will carry the voicings. If I can get more turbulence into the poems — and still balance the books — then there's life in them yet.

I'm not sure whether I should ask this question, but I'm curious about a general principle here so I'll ask it anyway. Do you think it is hazardous living with a poet?

Well! Doubtless after a season in hell with Rimbaud or Verlaine you might wind up in either hospital or jail . . . But, to misquote a phrase, mine have not been like Verlaine's and Rimbaud's. In fact, if I had to accuse myself of anything in this territory, it would be of not being able to live alone. I was already effectively co-habiting at the age of 19 and we were together for a little over twenty years. My second wife and I were already living together when the divorce came through. I've only really had two serious relationships in my life and those are they. I would say the hazards of living with me are not special to my writing poetry, aside from the risk that your name might end up in an acrostic. It's possible, though, that there's an unusual mental absenteeism that can be observed from time to time. Lots of blokes must be more of a hazard than me — and I've never had a relationship with a woman poet, so I can't comment on how it might be.

To take a trivial example, from reading your poems I have the suspicion that you are not quite as tidy as some of the people you have lived with. Poets being messy is not a hazard in itself, and you may in fact be an extremely tidy person. But in the Rosemary Laxton *sequence you appear not to meet certain exacting standards and this gives the poems a relaxed defiance. More recently, in 'Remembering February' somebody else's distress at the encroaching dust and clutter results in a fine stanza balancing mess and sense.*

Yes, with the two people I've lived with it may be me who accepts chaos more easily then they did and do. I'm from a family of three boys and a girl. We used to generate mess like breathing. My two daughters are much the same. In 'Remembering February' the exasperation is not mine — and neither is the mess — and I'm trying to mitigate it and its reverberations. In my first marriage there was a faint undercurrent of the old bourgeois-bohemian conflict, which doubtless was milked for an occasion or two. Perhaps, back then, I would have preferred to be living in an atelier rather than a sitting room — but poems like 'Dirty Language' and 'Living in the Workroom' get their dynamics from being on both sides of the quarrel at the same time. So there's a syncretic approach here too.

But do you think there is a cost attached to producing good poetry out of other peoples' frustrations, and should poets have domestic warnings attached? Or are they only writing down the things that everybody thinks and does anyway?

There may be a cost, but if you believe that poetry is a part of life and you're tempted to try and have poetry do as much in life as possible, then you've got to accept the potential cost to your friendships and loves. I've never concealed the fact that I write things, so I suppose you could say I have carried my own warning. Both of the people with whom I've lived were, in this sense, forewarned. My first wife used to say that even when the poems appeared to be about her, they were not: they were simply the poetry's representations. My second wife is too busy to read me. She's not a native speaker, and she has the person to understand. Being on both sides of these quarrels, if that's what they are (and a writer has to be to make such conflicts work) means that I'm trying not to use the poetry to score points or settle grudges. If poets should have government health warnings attached, then, perhaps, so should we all — governments included.

Your descriptions have a metaphysical conscience insisting through the shifts of perspective. The most mundane furniture can cue this conscience; I'm thinking of 'In the Background', where 'The length of close streets / goes unconfirmed by car noise', or 'Difficult Mornings' where 'there's barely time for last night's news / to stir me on this far side of the planet / with its aerial view of railway lines / running through a district in my home town / where a child's battered body had been found'. Do we need metaphysical poetry these days?

This reminds me of Davie's 'Or, Solitude' from the 1960s: 'The metaphysicality / Of poetry, how I need it! / And yet it was for years / What I refused to credit.' By a happy chance, one of the A-level texts for June 1971 was Helen Gardner's anthology of Metaphysical poets, and we were talked through those key poems in minute detail. So one answer to your question might be that I, at least, needed it in those days.

You have a delicate idea of what constitutes a metaphysical conscience: for me those two quotations are attempts to describe a situation as it happened to be. Like the view of the 'burning worlds' through the skylight in 'Pressure Cooker Noise', in Herschel

Road (whose name helped to prompt that bit of star gazing) the consciousness of space, distance, presence and absence, the vast contained in the small, and vice versa, that's how I feel myself aware of the world around. But in the more recent 'Winter Interiors' there's a routine acknowledgement that 'we are not all states, all princes'. Donne's strain of proud metaphysical self-centredness, I'm assuming some of us don't need.

So what kind of metaphysical assistance can poetry give us?

I recently found myself with the family in the Sendai planetarium, staring up at a model of the heavens with little lights flickering on and off, the music of the spheres on a sound track, and an explanatory voice-over in Japanese. It was like stumbling onto a ready-made poem — too much so perhaps. Anyway, I tried to rise to the occasion. Maybe some more continuously present senses of our true place in the vastness and the smallness of things would help us make better decisions and perform more beneficial acts at all levels of life — and even if that's only more pie-in-the-sky, who knows, it may nevertheless be one of poetry's possible roles to try and help maintain just such perspectives.

NINE

Left to their own devices

ADAM PIETTE: *Carcanet is bringing out a* Selected Poems *this year, which includes work from* The Benefit Forms *(1978) through* About Time Too *(2001) right up to the present. Was it difficult making the selections? Was there a sense of breaking up the considered sequences of your collections?*

Getting around four hundred pages of poetry into the one hundred and thirty text pages of the *Selected Poems* did mean losing some of that considered shape. In its place I composed 6 sections that attempt to be a set of considered sequences themselves. Each of them tries to represent the feel of the particular book or books. There are only a few longer works not represented at all: 'Going out to Vote' and 'Confetti', for example. I would like to republish my poem for John Wilkinson one day and with as minimal a revision as possible, but not quite yet. 'Confetti' is a work that, aside from the three parts republished in the *Liverpool Accents* anthology, needs to be reconsidered. In one or two crucial ways it has not comfortably outlived its painful occasion. I don't think it was exactly difficult making the selection, though. Michael Schmidt mentioned its being a possibility in 1997, so I've had plenty of time to ponder. The considered sequences of the collections just had to be temporarily sacrificed, but the poems are more or less kept in their order of appearance.

A great deal of your poetry is about the possibilities of reconsideration, the limits life and art must acknowledge when reworking past lived occasions. You have slightly revised many of the poems in the Selected, *and I was wondering how far the act of revision re-enacted the poems' own struggles.*

Years ago Giles Smith, then an undergraduate, pointed out to me that when I put 'fixing trays' about my grandpa's amateur photography in 'Granny, After Chardin' it was a mistake, because there's only one fixing tray. Phil Horne had questioned the grammar at the beginning of the third verse, because, in an attempt at relative self-effacement, I had perpetrated one of those trailing clauses which changes subject when you hit the main verb. This is the kind of help a poet like me needs. I'm very grateful to all the people who've noticed things like this. The minimal revisions to this piece are to remove those little flaws from a poem I'm very fond of. You've got to try and balance the claims of the lived occasions against those of the creative occasions while not leaving out of account various reading experiences. Doing the minimum necessary to respond to these often conflicting requirements is what post-publication revision has to be, in my view.

You've chosen Antonio Pollaiuolo's Daphne and Apollo *in the National Gallery as the cover for the selection, depicting the moment of Daphne's metamorphosis into the laurel tree with Apollo's vain grasp of the changing form, a mythological moment important to your poem 'The Happiness Plant', quoted from on the back cover. Is art for you (as it was for Ovid's Apollo) at its root always evocation and re-vision of the lost loved one?*

Umberto Saba wittily suggests in one of his aphorisms that Petrarch's Laura is actually his mother! That's why he can't have her. Rather differently, the second poem in my book, 'A Homage', ends with the sorry recognition that art might be driven not by an unachievable, but by a lost relation to your mother. There's a thread in my poems about that, which one critic stumbled on — in both senses — when inexactly describing a poem of mine as 'unfilial'. My mum suggested Chardin's 'The Schoolmistress' for the cover, but Carcanet didn't want it. I'd already asked for and been advised against Van Gogh's 'La Crau', another cover that would have pointed towards a family theme. That particular 'Apollo and Daphne', a weird picture that just flickered through my mind as I was writing 'The Happiness Plant', was my third choice. Poetry is said to live in its metaphors. If having the power to change one thing into another with language and imagination has to be paid for by the loss of the desired object — that might be a fair-ish bit of poetic justice. But, while you've of course touched on a key theme in art here, I would have to say that for me it isn't always the case. The 'Via Sauro Variations', for instance, narrate such a loss only to have it restored. There, Daphne, through the force of feeling and circumstance, turns back into a woman. Reader, I married her.

Your poem about a print of Van Gogh's La Crau *reads as a magical dream of stable relationship. Yet your father in the poem criticizes the sky for being too uniform. 'A Short History' is about the ways his voice dominated the industrial-suburban environment of your childhood, his parish, the zones of unemployment and decay in your first collections, where the sky writhes with 'power-lines'. How far is your early poetry a negotiation with your father's voice?*

My dad says 'That blue's not right' in the poem not only because he did say that the print didn't reproduce the colours well, but also because his remark suddenly chimed with a bit in Frank O'Hara's 'Steps' where 'I go by to check a slide and I say / that painting's not so blue'. If the word 'negotiation' means 'coming to terms with' and also 'coming through a narrow strait' then, yes, most of the early work contains something of this sort. I can think of various writers who have church backgrounds (my dad used to know Tim Parks'), and it may be that writing provides a means of both having and standing off from an authoritative voice. Devotion to the literary is a worldly way of having something like a spiritual vocation too. So you can follow in dad's footsteps, as it were, but not do the same thing he did. My critical interest in poetry and performative utterances derives in part from the fact that in the right circumstances he would 'Pronounce you man and wife', while poetry has no such writ in the world. But perhaps it's also worth saying that my real rebelling had all taken place long before the writing of those earlier poems. They seem more about an extended accommodatory aftermath of difficulties in childhood and youth, rather than a report on the negotiations themselves.

After the poems accommodating the aftermath of your father's influence, come the humbling poems about the aftermath of the rape in Italy. You have had to speak about and justify these poems enough, so maybe you could comment on a remark you made in interview to the effect that Vittorio Sereni (the poet you and Marcus Perryman have translated), born in the area north of Milan where the event took place, helped you 'transform a nightmarish sense of Italy into something more benevolent', a feeling that informs your poem 'Towards Levanto'. The bloody Italy of Titus Andronicus, *the Italy of the two world wars, your 'father's and grandfather's wars', the Italy of Salò, of Pound's* Pisan Cantos, *the Italy that sent Sereni to war and POW camps in Algeria and Morocco: how did Sereni help you out of the darkness of the Italy of history, of the Italy of that violation?*

Vittorio Sereni, a junior infantry officer at the time, was captured in Sicily in July 1943 and by 8 September he had been shipped to Oran. About the same time, my father crossed the Mediterranean in the opposite direction from Bizerta to Sicily in a landing craft. While

Pound was desperately compounding his errors by trying to broadcast propaganda for the Salò Republic and writing those two dreadful Cantos 72 and 73, my dad was interpreting captured maps in a Signals unit, commanded, if his memory is not mistaken, by a Captain Prince of the Intelligence Corps — author of 'Soldiers Bathing'. One of my dad's aerographs to his mother is quoted in part 4 of my 'More Aftershocks'. It was my dad's reminiscences of his time in Italy travelling right up to Brunik in the Alto Adige before the Armistice that fired my interest in the place and its culture. Studying Joyce's Trieste period, Pound's Italian enthusiasms and entanglements, and Adrian Stokes's writings came out of that. I encountered Sereni's name for the first time in 1979 and started to try and render some of his poems the following year. That's about the same time I started writing the sequence of poems about the rape.

The problem I was having with Pound is that, as I see it, in the *Pisan Cantos* the language, style, and voicing of the poem is not distinguishable from the catastrophically bad judgements about politics and fascism. Even the famous 'What thou lovest well' passage from the end of Canto 81 is a stubborn defence of his own politico-cultural position in 1945. What I needed was an example and an aesthetic attitude, in the broadest sense, which resisted the damage of such errors, not one stubbornly sticking with them. Sereni's work was a help. More personally, an effect of the rape was to rob us of our youth. Some of Sereni's poetry is about a similar robbery by circumstance. Frankly, I needed to be rescued and be allowed to rediscover a sense of the possible in life. 'Unfaithful Translations' and 'Towards Levanto' are poems attempting to bring together a renewed sense of possibility that I discovered by returning to Italy, by co-translating Sereni, and by meeting Ornella Trevisan, who was to become my second wife some ten years later. The second of these poems suspects the horrid fact that my recovery was not going to keep together the longstanding relationship with my first wife who had directly suffered that rape. If those poems are shamefully elusive or evasive, that's one possible reason why.

In 'Ventisei', Sereni's richly troubled and time-dense prose account of returning to Sicily with his family, revisiting the sites of his capture in 1943 twenty-six years later (translated by you and Marcus Perryman in the first issue of Numbers*), he talks about the ways lines by Cavafy were adopted by* *his returning imagination, helping him turn the unbearable circumstances remembered into impulses to create. How important are such strange friendly meetings for your poetry and translation work?*

I'm fairly wedded to the idea of inspiration coming from ordinary events and occasions, so a question might be why I'm not simply flooded with promptings for poetry on a daily basis. In practice, it isn't enough to have experiences or memories that could, conceivably, make a poem. There has to be a conjunction of event and memorable phrase. Words have to start forming themselves around the occasion. This can frequently begin with the return of a passage from a writer whose work you tend to live with anyway — the words of Francis Bacon's about those with sharp tongues being wary of those with long memories in 'Your Other Country', for example. Sometimes I've translated poems that have contributed to work of my own in this way — as if it were the least I could do in gratitude. One of the things I owe to 'Ventisei' is that, while working through a rough draft in the Dordogne in 1983, I began to glimpse a vague outline of how my own work in various adjacent fields might fit together as a whole.

Could you give us a sense of that vague outline?

My first sense of what I was doing shows in the early poems about leaving the north of England, and my unpublished PhD thesis called *Responsibilities and Distances.* That glimpse in 1983, the year Sereni died, was of what the next phase might really be about. Three published books are what show of it: *This Other Life* (1988), *Selected Poems of Vittorio Sereni* (1990), and *In the Circumstances: About Poems and Poets* (1992). All three are both committed to, and sceptical about, creative activity as a reparative emblem for culpability that is itself circumstantial, deriving from a complicit passivity. If I had been able to find a publisher for my novel, *September in the Rain*, and been able before the brain tumour crisis appeared to finish a book of studies called *Literary Rapes: Lucrece to Larkin*, then the outline might not have been quite so vague. I still haven't given up hope that they'll come out someday.

I wonder if we could talk a little about your very moving long poem about the brain tumour crisis, 'A Burning Head'. It's written in fifteen sections of 1 to 3 stanza blocks, predominantly in a 3 or 4 beat short line, though again rhythm is open to variation.

When I was working in Aberystwyth in 1981, I came across a copy of Montale's *Le occasioni* that a student had defaced by writing in the meanings of some words and then dumped in a second-hand bookshop. Ten years later my efforts to decipher his sequence of 'Mottetti' would come in rather useful. 'A Burning Head' borrows its title from Sereni's phrase 'il capo bruciante di dolore' — and that last word might be rendered as 'pain' or 'sorrow'. It's obviously not just about the operation. Those fifteen poems were written in such short sections partly because it was all I could manage. They were begun in the hospital in May 1993 and worked on through the convalescence during the summer. I certainly showed a version of the sequence to Ralph Pite in August and he made a number of suggestions. The last part was finished in Japan that autumn, and added even after the magazine publication, I recall. They were started by writing down, or asking people to write down at first, brief phrases or aids to memory that struck me while it was all going on. I was fearful that an operation on my brain might change me in some way, or even stop me being able to write poetry, so I began immediately as mental physiotherapy. That game old man's misunderstanding of the nurse's question ('How much can you stand?') was probably noted down as it happened.

The section form is one you'd used a long time before, notably with 'The Benefit Forms', and it's one you were to go on to use to notate complex memories, occluded narratives nearly, of love affairs ('Scargill House' and 'Via Sauro Variations') as well as difficult communications with the dead in the two earthquake poems ('Aftershocks' and 'More Aftershocks'). What is it about the form that worked for you when trying to represent these very different and taxing times? Is it a confessional form?

There's a conscious recall of 'The Benefit Forms' in 'A Burning Head'. They're both state of the welfare state poems. No, I don't think it's necessarily a confessional mode. The poems edit and reshape moments and experiences, bringing out significances and giving them directions . . . There's a moment in the 'Via Sauro Variations' where I paraphrase a line from Dante's 'Tre donne' canzone: 'if faults do die when they're confessed'. Even there I'm not exactly confessing, more commenting on the way your hurt loved ones may harbour grudges whatever you say. Occluded narrative is a good description of Montale's 'Mottetti', and I'm trying to learn from him how to keep a story going with only short glimpses. 'Scargill House' surprised me. It came from no more than the rhyme of 'palaver' and 'father' in 5 and 'lips' and 'Apocalypse' in 6. I wrote those two very short pieces and then got nothing more for about 6 months. One morning in early autumn I awoke with the memory of 7, composed a bit in my head, then got up and wrote it down. After that, the sequence began growing in both directions, discovering what more it might be about as it went along. 'Aftershocks' began with part 12 and was then composed more or less backwards. 'Via Sauro Variations' is more a work of revision and consolidation. It was in part assembled from various bits of poems that I had put aside, or decided were in need of revising — and then had a few additional parts composed for the evolving form. The thing I found useful about this way of working is that it's structurally both ambiguous and flexible. Are these song cycles, or sonnet sequences, or loose pindarick odes? Do the numbered parts make poems complete in their own right and then strung together, or are they not much more than stanzas? I managed to produce some quite sustained pieces (while having very little physical stamina, and then babies in the house) by not deciding about those sorts of question.

What helps the writing of these poems read as fruitfully ambiguous and flexible is their subtle and oblique representations of cultural, national and political 'burning' issues: the reference to the 'ghost of Joe Stalin' and ex-Yugoslavia in 'A Burning Head' complicating the welfare theme, the reflection on postwar collective memory in 'Aftershocks', the delicate allusions to post-industrial collapse in 'Scargill House'. Being non-aligned has not meant a retreat into the purely private (which does, incidentally, make me regret the non-inclusion of 'After Bansui', the poem from About Time Too *which interrogates both Audenesque engaged poetry and Japan's history).*

I'm glad you like 'After Bansui', though I'm not sure any of my work exactly shines a light in your eyes and announces that it has ways of making you talk! Another sequence unselected would be 'South Parade' occasioned by the Falklands events of 1982, but not published until four years later. There are many that will just have to wait for the publication of a *Collected Poems*. Is 'non-aligned' what those poems are? That's not my sense of the two occasioned by general elections: 'More About the Weather' and 'Red Wednesday', for instance. I'm not sure that culturally-speaking there's such a thing as the purely private. In 'Convalescent Days' the phrase 'domestic wars' might be understood to mean quarrels between husbands and wives, or, equally, the very bad news coming from the Balkans at that time. Neighbours are neighbours wherever they live. Poems like 'News Abroad' or 'Nabucco' are aligned and engaged, but not necessarily overtly so, and not always for any of the one or two options that are publicly on offer. Poems seem to me objects which in their best natures work to occasion and sponsor kinds of understanding relations, and are thus in themselves engaged in an endeavour not always closest to that unfolding in the day-to-day reactivities of political agendas. The great problem of political poetry is its forever preaching to the converted. I'm not interested in that. In fact, I'm keen to leave preaching to the clergy — which brings us back to my dad. At 82, he's still a dedicated reader of newspapers and commentator on current affairs programmes, by the way.

'Non-aligned' comes from you, in interview speaking of your situation as a poet between the exclusive Cambridge Poetry avant-garde and the fêted celeb poets of the London market. I'd like to pick up on your definition of poetry as an object that works to sponsor kinds of understanding relations. Many of your wittiest poems are about material objects in rooms and landscapes, objects that court surmise, arrange their environments and historical scapes in puzzling, febrile ways. They are images, clearly, but the poetry won't go too far down the conceptual road (as with Stevens' jar, or Williams' wheelbarrow) but insists on preserving the fact and materiality of the encounter. 'Coat Hanger', for instance, is a happy freewheeling reflection on your own use of images from the world. You see a coat hanger mysteriously dangling from a tree in Japan, and the poem turns round the wonderful coincidence that Jasper Johns, famous artist of the coat hanger, had been in Japan during the Korean War. The poem hints at other affinities between Johns' artisanal neo-Dada play with the common object and your practice?

Ah yes, I'm happy not to be on any of those pathetic maps of contemporary poetry sketching out the supposed territories of power and remark — in that sense I'm non-aligned. But if you want to know where my poetry stands on nuclear proliferation or weapons of mass destruction and, at the same time, on loving your enemy and doing good to those that hate you, all you need do is read 'These Last Days' or '23 January 1980'. Not only was Jasper Johns in Japan, he was quite possibly stationed at the US base that was on the exact site of the present arts faculty building where I have an office. In 'Coat Hanger', Williams' poem is directly alluded to — but where he has 'so much depends', I have 'so much else that could depend'; and I also had in mind that wonderful list and shrug at the end of Baudelaire's 'Le Cygne'. His is a poem about exile and change and survival, and so, in a different key, is mine. I think the method of the poem is probably 'happy free-wheeling'. I'm not sure that the themes are exactly that — Frank O'Hara's 'loneliness' on his destroyer in Miyagi Bay, off Sendai, in August 1945, Johns here during Korea painting posters warning GIs about VD, and me in the same place without my wife and family in 1997. There are images of body parts emerging from foliage 'like a phantom limb' also borrowed from other paintings by Johns. The poem hints at affective disturbances, the substitution of objects for feelings, disorientations caused by losses of emotional target, and behind them wars and occupations, and the survivals of customs for coping with crisis. I think of it as a reprise of themes and ways of working that I stumbled on with 'The Yellow Tank' six years before. Those two slightly uncharacteristic poems explore their themes in a way that seeks to replace obsession with objects by attachment to people, or to achieve attachment by working through obsession. If you think of the poems as objects too, then there's your trajectory towards the sponsorship of understanding relations.

In poems like 'The Explanation', 'Your Other Country', 'Playing Dead', 'The House Museum', 'Farther Adventures', you discover lines of feeling connecting ideas of home with the obliterations of time, the estrangements of memory and exile, the return of the native. These poems are counterpointed by your family poems — 'Winter Interiors', 'For My Daughter', 'Remembering February' — where home has other meanings, other loving modes. Has it been a luxury and a trial to have (and not have) two countries?

It's really three, if you count my wife's hometown of Parma, Italy, where we have an address and I am, technically, resident. The way you put it, a luxury and a trial, seems structurally right: I don't appear to be able to settle on a more balanced or integrated view of the situation. There are the benefits and the disbenefits, and they just co-exist, not apparently talking to each other. The benefit for the poems has, as you note, been the development of two sustained thematic variations — neither of which is much foreshadowed in the first decade or so of work written mostly in England. The two themes are related by the fact that the family has been an important part of my living outside my country of birth, both in that it wouldn't have come into existence if I'd stayed at home, and that I wouldn't have been able to stay away without their company and support.

There have been moments when it seemed as if living in three different places were a way forward, an internationalism of outlook and experience. Some of the poetry has that scope, perhaps. But the present moment is one in which travel is more frustrating, and the notion of a benign internationalism has been attacked from various points of the compass. There's also a sense in which it only appears a luxury to people who live in the same place, year in year out, and who only go away for a week or so on holiday. The different places in which we live have provided occasions for broadening the mind, it's true, but they are also merely diverse forms of the local that we happen variously to inhabit.

Skies, weather, islands, distances and directions, catalogues of local sights seen, your later poems sing a geography of the imagination with something of a German courting and resisting of melancholy, as with Heine, Hölderlin. The resistance is various and moving, but on the page takes the form of a reconnaissance and recrudescence of the various meanings of common phrase and key word, as with 'by the way' in 'By the Way'. On the page, the language is doing so much more than making 'the best of each new confusion'.

Those poems may have developed out of the ones like 'Difficult Mornings' and 'For my Daughter' which use a single line to set off variations on the theme. Brief idiomatic phrases can be turned, or unpacked, or taken literally as starting points for explorations whose points of arrival are guided by the idioms, but not determined by them. Yet every device of this sort is extremely vulnerable to hardening into a routine, and after exploring the possibilities in a few poems, of which 'By the Way' is one of my favourites, I more or less stopped. It's still there in the technique locker, though, waiting an occasion to be dusted off. You mention Heine. I recall lucklessly trying to find rhymes to translate his sad little exile poem 'In der Fremde', about being kissed by the German language. My poems grown out of common English phrases perhaps resist the melancholy of distance and isolation by appearing to be gifted by the language itself. It's the English language that has given me my job and vocation. Speaking of being kissed, it was in an English language class that I first met my wife. Poets can learn a lot about their medium by hearing it as through the ears of a non-native speaker. What you describe as 'doing so much more' may be one of the underlying strategies of poetry. On the surface, you claim to be making the best of a bad job, or to be pointing out the limits to what can be done ('I'd only make amends', for example). Then, without claiming anything, you try to complete a work which demonstrates and manifests something almost miraculously more than could ever be claimed — and the only people who can know or say whether or how the poem has achieved it are its long-term, fully-engaged readers.

In Poetry, Poets, Readers: Making Things Happen, you distinguish your own view of the relation of poetry to circumstance and action from the severe ethical line on errors, mistakes and faux pas taken by Christopher Ricks, Eric Griffiths and Geoffrey Hill, three dominant figures at Cambridge when you were there in the 1980s. To a certain extent, this act of discrimination repeats your earlier disengagement from the poets of the Cambridge school gathered round Perfect Bound. *Yet from another point of view, your work, critical and poetic, has evolved a language of fine discrimination which owes some things to both of these two schools, if only in the music of its divisions, how it thrives, locally, 'being left to its own devices', how it makes things out of language in ways Roy Fisher demonstrated, and has the tactfulness of the printed page in ways William Empson taught and admired.*

Back in 1977, being interviewed in a side room of the Union Chambers, Roy Fisher responded to a brief interjection of mine by saying: 'Any bully boy thing is out for me, whether it's an atavisitic bully boy, or a nostalgic one, or an academic one, or one that comes out of modernism. You can have bully boys in that just as well.' My homage poem for him, 'Playing Dead', reaches towards a close with a catalogue of fears from my industrial slum childhood: 'policemen and dark alleys, / railway lines, the waste ground, / talking to strangers, school bullies —'. I'm not physically big, and I was brought up to understand violence, so as to avoid resorting to it. Being the local vicar's son, and a bit clever, I got bullied and had to learn how to keep away from dangerous people. What I didn't expect, and so didn't learn well enough, was how to spot at sight an intellectual bully.

One of the things that Empson didn't like about Christianity was the justification some of its manifestations seem to provide for 'torture worship' — the religious bully boy. Two Cambridge-based projects which, from the outside, may have looked like useful and fairly successful bits of ancillary work for poetry and poets — *Perfect Bound*, and the critical collection *Geoffrey Hill: Essays on his Work* — produced quite a bit of grief for me when young and socially vulnerable. In so far as it was possible, I had to put a certain distance between myself and both of those more secure circles of power and influence. But I should add that, in my case, being attuned to making poems from atmospheres, from the air of occasion and circumstance, also means being touchy and sensitive. I've tried hard to learn as much as I could from the people you mention. But I've needed to preserve a certain independence so as to avoid, as far as possible, being absorbed into someone else's game, suffering the debilitating effects of persecutory righteousness, or the expressed and would-be self-fulfilling assumption that you'll never amount to anything, or the *Schadenfreude* that greets every public slip-up you inevitably make.

After all, if you have, or think you have, some modicum of talent — but also know that you are a provincial and a slow-starter with, as a result, little access to power and preferment — you are required either to wear the cap and bells at court, or get used to the wilderness. I've been learning to thrive like the rosebay willowherb on a railway-line embankment because, when it comes to 'the mystery of things', you don't usually have much of a choice.

Looking more broadly at the role and function of Selected Poems *in the lives of poets, one could argue that they give poets not only an opportunity to present their wares, as it were, but also to chart the times their collections have travelled through, at all kinds of private and historical levels. Your writing career has seen and responded to the force and demise of the Cold War in 1989-1992, the shift from generational wartime memory (as with your father and Sereni) to generational postwar memory, all the unprecedented changes undergone by British culture. Has the collection allowed you yourself to take stock in these ways?*

Well, yes, I'm conscious of these things happening and of time passing too. Reading over the proofs of the book I naturally wondered about the extent to which the occasioning contexts had evaporated, or had remained much the same. Some views of the north of England, for example, don't now recall the industrial decay and penury of 'The Benefit Forms' and 'Some Hope' — but others still do, and 'The

Relapses' scouts some of those similarities and differences. The sharpest sensation of change came when checking 'In the Small Hours', written in 1983, with its line reporting a moment in a dream where I'm accused of 'slandering a Warsaw Pact state.' The thought flickered across my mind that the phrase would soon be in need of a footnote! But I don't think putting the collection together exactly made me take stock of those things. After all, I'd been taking stock of them when I was writing the poems. Still, time brings in its revenges. Just now I've been experiencing the curious sensation that my poems are — for the time being, anyway — doing better at surviving than the Soviet Union, the Warsaw Pact, heavy industry in the British Isles, Yugoslavia, some tyrants, some political and literary reputations, and, sadly, my first marriage. That's one of the things you have to like about poetry, though. With luck, it's got time on its side.

TEN

Aphorisms as poetry or criticism?

ALEX PESTELL: *Your most recent work of non-criticism is a book of aphorisms and prose poems. Could you say something about how these forms interact with your other work, the poetry and the criticism? Should we read them as marginalia to the poetry, footnotes to the criticism?*

They could be read as both or either of those things, and as neither. *Untitled Deeds* is in three parts. The third one contains poems in prose, a couple of which date back to the 1970s and were written as experiments alongside differently lineated ones I was making in those years. Among the large number of others I've read, the three twentieth-century poets who have taught me most must be Pierre Reverdy, Vittorio Sereni, and Roy Fisher. They have all written imaginative prose, and prose poems, alongside or as part of their poetry. Though I hadn't published a poem in prose since 1980, that didn't mean I'd given up on the idea or the form. They're simply poems without line endings. Part two, 'The Draft Will', began life as a memoir back in 1993-4. It was the first piece of writing in which I began to explore the ways that speech acts might impact, or have impacted, on my father's family. So it comes before the critical writings that went into *Poetry, Poets, Readers: Making Things Happen*. The short sections were focused and revised for a projected small press publication in the form of a series of postcards attached to each other in concertina form. The publication never materialized; but the revision served thoroughly to define the piece and I kept it. The aphorisms were the most unexpected of all. They just began to accumulate quickly during 2002-3 — though some of them derive from earlier occasional pieces. I like the form, in as much as it is a single form. I've continued to jot them down in my notebook when one comes into my head. Some of them are like short prose poems, a few are haiku laid out without line breaks. Some are paragraphs of remarks. Others are aphorisms in the Oscar Wilde or Karl Kraus sense of the term. I find that when I pick up the book and dip into it, I tend to read them for what they are.

Though you have criticized elsewhere the binarism that characterizes the 'avant-garde' vs 'mainstream' debate, you were early on involved with writers who have subsequently received scant attention from the larger publishing houses. Has their approach to poetry influenced you?

One of the reasons why I criticized that stubborn binarism is because, as well as the three just named, I've been influenced by a great many poets, living and dead, English-speaking and in other languages. The large publishing houses don't, any more, have much time or space for contemporary poetry, and only tend to publish poets that they think they can sell in numbers that will make the decision seem justified higher up the corporation. It would be difficult, I think, to develop a real sense of what is being done, or might be done, in poetry now by attending only to the lucky few who write what the larger publishers feel they can risk trading in. I'm not sure I can really say if the other ones and their approach to poetry have influenced me. Some have a bit, and others haven't. They are such a various crowd, and hardly see eye to eye on anything anyway.

There seems to be little regard, on either side of the arbitrary dividing line between avant-garde and mainstream, for the methods of the opposite camp, which is, perhaps, dispiriting. Do you see any possibility of dialogue between the two?

Granting for the sake of our conversation that there are such 'camps', I see possibilities in the hearts and minds of sensitive and intelligent readers or writers who can appreciate varieties of human behaviour, intelligence, and feeling. I thought that the two young editors of *Poetry Review*, who completed their stint earlier this year, tried their best to encourage such dialogues. There are entrenched interests on both sides of the supposed line, and they will not only insist that there is a line but that only those on one side or the other can be with the angels. There's a lot of this 'divide and rule' kind of thing in the world . . . But I don't think poetry and those involved with it should be mimicking such destructive discrimination.

In Untitled Deeds, *you disparage Geoffrey Hill's comment that 'tyranny requires simplification' as a simplification itself. There seem to be at least two kinds of difficulty in poetry, the sort you find in Hill's work, which is often ultimately resolvable after a certain amount of legwork, and the sort found, e.g. in J. H. Prynne's, which seems to require a different kind of attention. Would you go along with this proposition, and how much work can a poet properly ask of his or her readers?*

Hill's comment is not only that tyranny requires simplification, but also that difficulty is properly democratic. It's the entire complex proposition that strikes me as polemically simplifying a large number of interrelated issues. One simplification is the tacit shift from talking about politics and propaganda, to talking about simple and complex poetic surfaces. Can we take one area to be a direct analogy of the other? I doubt it. But sticking with poetry . . . Prynne's supporters think his work is resolvable with effort. With critical help, or a search engine and some reference books, most of the difficulty you're talking about can be handled. The issue with much more recent poetry seems to me the relation between the elaborations of the language, the implied sensibility and attitudes of the writer, and the assumed relationship, however attenuated, with readers and the world at large. In such a context, Sylvia Plath is very difficult; Geoffrey Hill is painfully difficult; and Jeremy Prynne's difficulties have been all but edited out of existence. I myself don't think that poets can ask their readers to do any work at all. They can invite an attention to and understanding of their work that, if sufficiently gripping and rewarding, will draw further information and knowledge into that relationship.

I agree that reference works and the internet deal with the allusiveness of Hill and Prynne, but isn't there a more fundamental difference, in that the syntactic coherence and (usually) stable authorial voice of Hill is within the range of most readers' frames of reference, while so-called 'innovative' poetry questions assumptions about the uses of language through its refractory forms rather than through perhaps more intelligible argument?

That's certainly the defence, and one of the justifications, for some versions of 'innovative' poetry. The books of Prynne's that I read most closely and repeatedly were the ones published between the mid-1960s and the mid-1970s. In *Kitchen Poems*, *The White Stones*, and *Brass*, for instance, there is the sound of an authorial voice and some urgency in the address that suggests an aim to communicate information, value, and a view (or views) of the world. The styles which are justified on the grounds that they 'question' something by means of formal disruption insinuate a degree of exasperation about the condition of the world, reader expectations of poetry, and the contamination of communication between readers and writers that — while I can sympathize with, and appreciate the reasons for the exasperation

— I can hardly believe that the therapy does more than aggravate the problems. One trouble with this sort of 'questioning' is that its hidden agenda of assumed answers can be, thanks to the method, left unaddressed. However, poets have to follow out what they take to be the track of their inspiration, and follow it where it goes. If readers don't care to follow them, that may be no one's problem. If you're somehow suggesting there is a rule that means Prynne should not write as he sees fit, then I can't imagine what it would be. If you mean that you don't find it congenial, then there are plenty who will see eye to eye with you.

I'm not positing the existence of a 'rule', but I was wondering whether a lack of congeniality was perhaps a bracing or necessary antidote to more marketable poetry which, according to the argument cited above, is too complicit with the interests of those who have power, though I note that you have elsewhere poured cold water on the notion that left-wing politics finds its correlative in avant-garde formalisms.

We're each of us to some degree or other complicit with those who have power. Writing a curiously asyntactical, dictionally heterogeneous, or oddly lineated bit of text has practically no relation to that difficult fact. It can perhaps signal the desire to be less complicit; but it doesn't in itself make you any less so. Since true and good poetry of any kind has such a Cinderella relationship with real power, I can see the politico-scholastic interest in calibrating its degrees of complicity — but it shouldn't perhaps be confused with a commitment to reading or writing poetry itself. As for left-wing politics and avant-garde formalisms, I am not alone in noting the embarrassing fact of Pound's literary and political complexities — nor of noting Brecht's. As for congeniality, or a lack of it, I assume that people read because, in some crucial way, they like what they are doing. Wilde said that James wrote novels as if it were a painful duty. But he was of course referring to the feeling he got from reading them. I take it that people who buy James novels and dwell on them do it because they don't agree with Wilde. Perhaps I'm just saying that few, if any, read for the rather masochistic reason that we need a bracing antidote; and, if we sometimes do, taking medicine is only sensible when you are unwell. The 'bracing' aspect of rebarbative styles is likely, one way or another, to wear off fairly quickly. Reading things that feel somehow uncongenial at first sight might be a good way to try and grow, though.

As a poet who has, in addition to reviews, published three volumes of criticism, what importance to you attach to the role of criticism in the practice of poetry? How important is it that a poet theorize about his own practice?

I've said elsewhere that the desire to write poems and the capacity to finish ones, occasionally, that were acceptable to magazine editors, was something that came to me before I had worked out how to produce publishable reviews, and critical essays took even longer to learn. I recently read a remark to the effect that Wallace Stevens wrote criticism, when he did, to discover poetry. That makes sense to me. One way to put it might be that I have instincts and preferences and even obsessions about what I feel I can and can't do in poems, and writing criticism is one tool I have for finding my way around these 'tastes' as they impact upon my reading. It's also an opportunity to challenge and revise my own limits. If poets are theorizing after the fact of having written and published poetry, then it may be a harmless hobby. If they are constructing the theory before getting started I fear it may be a preemptive strike against making useful discoveries about themselves.

So does a critical essay sometimes act as a conduit between your reading and your writing, perhaps informing a conversation between your writing and tradition?

Yes, it almost always does. A critical essay can act as a conduit for stocking my mind in unforeseeable preparation for some future poem. It can also function as a spur to writing a poem — in the simple sense that I can become fairly disaffected with the business of pushing words around on a screen to describe and comment on someone else's already written poem. The blank pages of my notebooks or my blue and red pens can then start to seem like a tempting resort.

You have written that 'When the poems are read by others, and by those involved, the real situations alter again. Thus, as I do it, poetry becomes a part of life'. This is poetry as speech act, and as such is implicated in issues of faith and authority. Do you find it difficult to maintain faith in an art form which, due to lack of readers, risks becoming marginalized?

Well, there are two things here. I was talking in that aphorism about the way in which a poem might be received in an individual life, altering it and those around it, and helping to create the situations from which other poems might come. You only need a few real readers to experience those sorts of processes. I have no doubt that poetry can still be received in precisely this way. The other thing is that those words 'faith' and 'authority' seem too close to the terms of an established religion to have much connection with poetry's informal relations to readers, as I see them. Besides, the margins are, after all, as good a place as any, and probably better than some, for doing something different and perhaps lasting in the arts.

I was thinking of the means a writer might employ to alter 'real situation', which impacts upon the question of why writers write poetry, as opposed to, for example, fiction. Does 'poetry make nothing happen'?

Well, as I say, I've written a critical book called *Poetry, Poets, Readers: Making Things Happen.* I wrote the book to look again at Auden's claim and to lay it to rest. I have no doubt that poetry makes things happen — in the sense that as a human implement it can be used by people to effect how some of us think and feel — and so act. Nobody would raise the question of whether or not a letter can make things happen, would they? Think of the function of the letter at the end of *Persuasion*; but then think, too, of the way in which Captain Benwick is using poetry. He's a very useful character for Austen, and essential for Anne (even if she does recommend that he reads less of it). After all, it's he who settles Louisa Musgrove's fate — Anne's apparent rival for Captain Wentworth. The book seems to hint that Benwick's feelings are transferable from the dead Fanny because he's a poetry addict. How fortunate for the plot, and what it makes happen, that he is one. All that has to take place for poetry to make things happen is for those involved to read it as a form of fully meant and thoroughly embodied communication. Novels are not usually communications of quite this kind; and poetry's relation to the fictive is both more thoroughgoing and more patently conventional. That's why poetry can be more directly about, and directed towards, lived and living occasions. My book is an argument for holding fast to what people may naturally be inclined to do anyway.

The long poem, or sequence of poems, seems to be more in evidence the further into your career we look; for example 'A Burning Head', 'Aftershocks' or 'Via Sauro Variations'. Does the initial impetus to write a long poem somehow feel qualitatively different from that which kick-starts a shorter piece?

Yes, I think it probably does . . . But the three sequences you've just mentioned developed in very different ways: the first was an attempt to write my way through the first phases of a difficult convalescence taking any tiny memory of the period in hospital and then building it up into a little lyric while waiting around to feel better; the second began with the last piece and was built backwards, very quickly, rather like a shorter poem made of separate instances, and the last is a collage made up of poems, or bits of poems, written over the space of a decade and then revised. Something similar is true of *There are Avenues*— my longest work to dates, due out from the Brodie Press early in 2006. So I would tend to think that every poem, of whatever kind, has a different form of inspiration and growth. But yes, shorter poems seem like a little knot of feeling with an occasion that needs to be explored and then pushed along to create something additional somewhere else. Longer pieces have more knots, more interrelations, and their trajectory is likely to take in more points — so the preliminary sense of a burden must necessarily be more various or complex.

Does this 'sense of a burden' ever result in a complete poem in one draft, or is it necessary to work through the poem for several drafts before it's finished?

It strikes me as so rare as to be practically never that I've been able to write a poem in one draft. I may have been able to complete one in a single sitting, as it were; but that would probably involve three or four quickly written different versions of the piece. What most usually happens is that the burden is signaled by a few words, a phrase that someone says, a draft title . . . whatever. From this germ, which might be only an aid to memory, or might be a key part of the poem, I'm able, with luck and time, to use it as a sort of magnet for other phrases and bits of evocation — until the poem-to-be starts to define itself in the air and on the paper. The burden is the urge or the need that is then converted into something else in the process of work, in such a way as to disappear with the completion of the poem. I suppose that learning to write poetry, and, what's more, to enjoy writing it, means learning how to behave in relation to words such that the work produced then mysteriously matches, by supplanting it, that inchoate burden.

What role does diction have in your poetry? Could you say something about the issues involved in maintaining a coherent, often first-person voice within the bounds dictated by often strict forms?

These aren't things that I've ever thought much about as matters to be addressed in isolation. I write in a way that feels faithful to things in the world including myself, and I use the words that seem to do that best, to my ear. I've never had any great difficulty with first-person voice and form. The first poem of mine that I liked at all contains the line, repeated in each verse, 'for myself I only remember'. I have tended more to put my efforts into including dialogue, or interlocutors, or implied remarks that are prompting what the poem's voice utters. I think I'm saying that the issues are all in making sure that the coherence, such as it is, is shot through with materials and issues, and that the first-person is not shutting out the world. I recently read a comment by Luciano Erba to the effect that the first-person subject is 'dribbled' by the objects in the poem. Perhaps it's even kicked into touch by them sometimes. I'm as happy with a poem that doesn't have an 'I' in it as with one that does, unless there is an air that it's being left out for the wrong reasons, and then I put it back in.

When do you think the reasons for omitting the 'I' would be wrong?

When I was a very young writer, but one criticized enough to have become self-conscious, I could be tempted to write a lyric poem in the third-person, or to go out of my way to make a direct experience seem impersonal. Then a way of writing which would naturally include an 'I' — as the dramatic device for deploying the poem's experience — would be short-circuited by the sorts of critical or, worse, theoretical self-consciousness, I've just suggested. That would be one wrong reason. Another would be when you have a view or sense of things to articulate, one that contains something quite contentious, say, and from rhetorical defensiveness you formulate this abstractly, or you attribute it to a fictional 'we', or a stooge-like 'you'— or build it into some person-less writing. Then, to my mind, the poem is likely to come more alive, and be fairer too, if you allow a first-person subject to carry the can for what's going on. Don't get me wrong. It's not a question of being more or less true to the real me. The pronouns are part of the poet's toolbox; they need to be used with skill for the right sorts of job.

Insofar as you are both an academic and a poet, you are characteristic of so many published British poets, of whatever formal persuasion. What do you think of the relationship between these two spheres? Does the one inhibit the other?

The word 'poet' is an honorific, not a job description (as comparisons between what different poets do makes obvious). An 'academic' is someone who works in a teaching and research role in an academy. That is a sort of job description — though not necessarily a very specific one. If you teach a creative writing course, you need not be a writer; so there's still no necessary link between the spheres. I would have to say, I think, that there is no real connection between them. Maybe poetry isn't even a 'sphere'. It's an obsession. If your inspiration or need to write poetry is not very strong, then being a busy academic may well drive away the time and occasion that you could have found for your slight vein. If poetry is what you absolutely have to do, then it won't. At present I teach in a private women's university, one owned by a Buddhist temple in Kyoto. It's my way of funding a family life, and does allow time for my own work. As I say, the margins can be a productive place from which to operate. That's how it's been for me.

ELEVEN

There are avenues, aren't there?

TOM PHILLIPS: *This year sees you publishing two new books,* Ghost Characters *(Shoestring Press, 2006) and* There are Avenues *(Brodie Press, 2006). The latter is a single poem exploring, for the most part, biographically older territories. It's a 'long' poem and one which, as you explain in your author's note, was written on and off over a period of about twenty years. Could you elaborate on what you say in the note about the process of its composition or evolution?*

At the heart of that poem is a domestic quarrel between my mother and a family friend (now dead) — a woman who we had got to know when I was a little boy. She was a parishioner of my father's and stayed in touch with us, helping my mother with chores and other things. Shadows of this matter appear in 'Faith in the City' from *This Other Life* and 'Confetti' from *Entertaining Fate*. The person involved is also mentioned in 'Liverpool . . . of all places', my memoir in the *Liverpool Accents* anthology. The quarrel in itself is no longer of any significance; but its reverberations for me have been long-lasting, and with branching echoes. The passage about the sheets of newspaper on the wiped kitchen floor focused those memories, and may have been drafted either as a part of, or spinning off from, some early parts of 'Confetti' in *Entertaining Fates*. There are a few other lines elsewhere in the poem that were drafted for that sequence, and then removed from it. So the poem began as something about my mother and me. Also essential for its evolution was the move my parents made just a mile or so up the road from the vicarage when my dad retired. Unlike almost all my other Liverpool-located poems (except 'The Relapses' in *Selected Poems* — which I did wonder about including in this poem, but eventually felt that it had defined itself as something different), *There are Avenues* is about returning to parents in their old age. Living in Japan has made such visits both more important and stranger. Sensations would occur, and I would try to write a bit of poetry about them — but, as I say in the note, those candidate poems would feel unfinished.

Was there any particular reason you decided to publish it separately rather than as part of Ghost Characters?

The poem is certainly related to two poems from the *Ghost Characters* work — 'Exchange Values', which includes a detail about Paul McCartney's house and Japanese tourists, and 'The Relapses' (in *Selected Poems*), occasioned by my and my mother's stays in Liverpool hospitals. There are a couple of other family-related poems too, so I suppose it could have been located somehow as a section in that book. The thought never crossed my mind. The material in the poem covers such a long period of time, and some of the sections have existed more or less untouched since the late 1980s, whereas the *Ghost Characters* poems are almost all from between approximately 1998 and 2001. So, for me, it's the book of my poems from that time, while *There are Avenues* is the summing up of a much longer involvement with a specific place.

So how and when did you realize that its various parts were tending towards a larger whole? Did the idea of its structure make a difference to the way it was written, particularly in the final drafts?

Maybe writing 'The Relapses' had something to do with it. That poem began towards the end of one summer, and then unexpectedly took off when we returned to Sendai, reaching a length that is fairly unusual for me. It made me look back at related drafts that were lying around, and at a couple of things published in the early 1990s but not collected. There were basically two ideas for how the parts would be put together. One was to have each stanza as a numbered section of the piece; the other was to have a set of parts with different numbers of stanzas in each one. The first idea disguised the real nature of the material and so had to be abandoned. Once the structure was settled, I revised or expanded some of the parts, leaving some of the others more or less as they were. At a certain point quite near the end of that process, it began to feel as if I were no longer assembling the poem, but polishing it.

In describing There are Avenues *as a 'long' poem, of course, I'm aware that in comparison with, say,* Four Quartets *(let alone a narrative like 'The Rime of the Ancient Mariner' or an epic like* Paradise Lost*), it's relatively short. What I mean, I suppose, is that it'll be seen as 'long' and I wonder whether you think this tendency to categorize just about anything over 40 lines as 'long' (or at least 'lengthy') nowadays reflects a kind of wariness — perhaps a justifiable scepticism — about possibilities of scale and the scope of contemporary poetry in general? And if so, where do you think* *that might have come from? Is this a legacy of modernism's obsession with 'form', for example?*

No, I wouldn't claim it as a long poem exactly. It's just the longest piece I've been able to do so far. It's a sequence of slightly longer poems that contain snatches of narrative. Perhaps the best way to put this would be to say that the kinds of poems I tend to enjoy reading or writing have a structure that can be experienced as a continuously focused local cohesion. It's harder to maintain that over a larger canvas, and for me many of the longer modernist poems don't amount to a satisfying read for this reason. This is not a criticism of them, but a description of what I like. It would be a pleasure to feel that a poem of the kind I enjoy writing could be sustained over a longer span — but the conditions, whether cultural or personal, don't make it a possibility for me at the moment. If it doesn't come, it can't be forced. Still, I'm always interested in extending my range, whether by writing longer or shorter pieces — and what can't be forced may perhaps be coaxed. But there are long poems around now, poems very different from this one, like the book by Vikram Seth in the Pushkin stanza, or the ones by Les Murray, Derek Walcott, or Simon Armitage, and so on.

I'm glad to see a poet actually admit he enjoys writing (and reading) poetry! So many writers talk about writing as if it's a chore that they'd rather not do but, sorry, they can't help it. Or as if it's something so personal, so traumatic, it has to be dredged up — rather painfully — from the depths of their soul: an operation without an anesthetic. I suppose, for the most part, they're exaggerating for effect . . . or feel they have to do this to get their poetry taken seriously.

Nobody's forcing me to write poetry; and I assume that if I didn't enjoy this way of life then I would have not been able to continue with it. In my case, anyway, I can't see one reason to deny that I enjoy both of these activities, though that isn't incompatible, again in my case, with their being sometimes difficult or trying . . . Maybe the fact that easy things don't produce as much pleasure can be accepted without having to admit that poets must be masochists — or that only masochism justifies serious attention. What you describe is, of course, the faded version of an attitude patented during the Romantic era.

Back to specifics . . . In terms of its geography There are Avenues *returns to*

*Liverpool where you lived in the late 60s with your parents and presumably
its 'occasions' are return visits you've made at various times of your life.
Given, though, that you've lived in quite a few other places, are there any
aspects of these Liverpudlian 'territories' that made you want to write
about them in particular? What is it about this personal terrain that drew
you to it in this instance? Perhaps you could expand on what you say in the
author's note about the places and occasions of the poem?*

Leaving aside any personal and family associations I might have with
the place (in so far as that's possible) from having grown up there
and returned to it so often, what struck me about that area of South
Liverpool as soon as we moved there was the interplay of horizontals
and verticals. This shows up in all the poems, but especially the rather
abstractly schematized 'In the Background' from *Overdrawn Account*.
It's a mildly undulating bit of plain near the Mersey estuary. Some of
the old working-class parts of it had been entirely deforested. The
only verticals are the streetlamps and the flat fronts of terraces. The
lower middle- and middle-class parts are strikingly different, in that it
used to be part of Lord Derby's estate and is faintly rolling parkland
overlaid with detached and semi-detached housing. The social range
within a very small area is extreme — from the nakedly poor streets of
Garston's old port area, to architect-designed houses and bungalows
built in the sixties for Brian Epstein or Rita Tushingham's mum. I
didn't fall in love with it at first sight; in fact, when we first moved, I
didn't want to be there at all. I hated the endlessly similar avenues and
the shameful contrasts, as they seemed to me, of rich and poor. The
Wigan I had been living in for the past five years, a place where I'd left
behind friends and first sexual experiences, was more homogeneously
nineteenth-century urban poor. George Orwell refers to the brave
new housing of Speke in *The Road to Wigan Pier*. Then, as you say,
in the second half of the 1960s I quickly developed a complex set of
feelings for those stretches of south Liverpool, one that has been and
probably remains artistically formative.

*When you lived there, too, I imagine that Liverpool, like Bristol and
all Britain's ports for that matter, was beginning to show the signs of
the economic decline that would culminate in the late 70s and early 80s
depression, an industrial city becoming a post-industrial one. Were you
aware of that at the time?*

That's more or less the contextual story of my childhood. My mother is from South Shields, at the mouth of the Tyne. My early years are full of ships' hooters, shipbuilders' hammers and welding torches, ferries across rivers, cranes emptying holds . . . It wasn't until I came to Japan and visited Hong Kong that I caught a glimpse again of what that ship-filled world had felt like. Fast-forwarding, the Toxteth riots of 1981 get into the end of the poem called 'A Summer Thunderstorm' in *This Other Life*, as does that process of decay and change in poems about my father's parish from the first part of the same book.

As well as this, though, the new poem's also a 'return' in the sense that you've written about some of these places and people before — in poems in Overdrawn Account, *for instance, where the 'landmark' aerodrome, gasworks and reservations also appear — and, in some ways, it reminds me of 'Via Sauro Variations' on that score, an act of renegotiation with experience and how you've expressed it before. And, of course, you've used titles like 'There Again', 'More About The Weather', 'More Borrowed Scenery' . . . The idea of 'going back' seems central to your work.*

It is. That seems to be one process art is for me — a going back over things to relive them in such a way as to find another way out of them. It's as if I want to create the future by restructuring the past, or perhaps to re-understand the past so as to see how it led into the situation from which it's being reviewed. The multiple perspectives are temporal as well as spatial ones.

Sometimes, I suppose, that can get a bit disorientating for the reader — there's a surface confusion about which perspective we're getting or who's being addressed or who pronouns relate to. I know you've attracted comment on this sort of thing before but presumably it's not a deliberate attempt to mystify, rather a passing over of details that you don't consider pertinent?

There's always a dilemma in poetry about compounding and expounding. If everything is explained, it's not an experience of discovery for the reader. If not enough is at least occasioned and prepared for with an explanatory air, then there may well not be sufficient footing for that same reader. I wouldn't claim to have a magic formula as far as this dilemma is concerned; and, since every new poem sets the problem in its own terms, I wouldn't expect there to be such a formula. Doubtless some part of me thinks that a little bit of disorientation in art refreshes things, so I must expect readers that can cope with, and enjoy, being slightly disorientated — and, as you say, it's a surface confusion which would either clear up on rereading, or would remain as a feature of the text that we all just have to learn to live with, if we like the poem sufficiently to want to live with it.

You also seem to be 'mapping' several different 'Liverpools' in There are Avenues: *the public one (birthplace of the Beatles, a street which might 'stand for . . . the whole class system's rise and fall'), and a more personal one 'daubed with privacies' being the most obvious. Was this idea and the tension between different geographies — personal, public, other people's — something you were conscious of exploring?*

I think you can detect that starting in the would-be multi-perspective style of 'In the Background' and the three different 'takes' on a theme of 'Faith in the City'. So it's not only something I was consciously exploring in this poem; it's always there for me. The public and the private are interconnecting spaces in the social geography of life. Perhaps it's an aspect of my subjectivity that I understand it as such only and because I take it that there are other subjectivities, including ones that are more, or less, shared. Poetry for me might be one of the places in which such differences can be registered without the usual editing out of the intensely singular — something that contemporary societies, however much they may formally deny it, appear to have fairly little real interest in, or use for.

That's a long way from saying that poetry's simply a refuge for individual expression, though, isn't it?

Yes it is. By 'intensely singular' I assume 'in art' — where I don't think there is such a thing as 'individual expression' in that wholly solitary sense. Art is a social practice. It's learned by example from the living and the dead. For individual experience or feeling to be expressed as art, it has to find itself significantly among an entire culture of techniques, expectations, assumptions, and the like. This is one of the reasons why a successful poem can be more socially embedded, integrated, and also mobile than many an ordinarily sociable person. After all, it may be able to speak to readers not yet even born.

Early on in the poem you also wonder — in relation to McCartney's house — how celebrity could change 'this nondescriptness'. Doesn't poetry also change 'nondescriptness', paradoxically, by describing it? And is there an anxiety about that which, perhaps, fuels the end of the first section (the stanza beginning 'No, it's not that I mean to condemn . . .') and, perhaps more tangentially, the line later on about being 'lost before things in themselves', an anxiety about the relationship between words and things and, for that matter, poets?

Some of that is jet lag and reverse culture shock. These days we come in from the other side of the world, take a twelve-hour flight to Copenhagen or Frankfurt, then we hang around in the airport until the shuttle hop to Manchester leaves. Then, at about seven or eight at night, in England, and three in the morning in Japan, we are taxied to Liverpool. Those arrivals have a lunar weirdness, and the passage in which the phrase 'there are avenues' appears is just such an arrival with a glimpse of the moon through clouds. So I'm registering all sorts of disorientations and defamiliarizations. But, I suppose, I don't need to do any of that 'making strange' business. I frequently find myself baffled by the simple existence and ordinary arrangements of things. My style has evolved in the hope of registering that feeling, and trying to reproduce it by making things musically vivid, while, simultaneously, composing those things into a shape that carries meanings — not forgetting, of course, that the freshly meaningful in poetry has to find its sources in places where meaning is scarce — in 'the nondescript', for instance.

In a way, then, it's a poem that's as much 'about' your being in Japan as it is about Liverpool?

Undoubtedly . . . I started trying to write the sections in which my mother figures exactly as I was leaving the country in 1989. Living outside of England has brought me closer to my parents, and so to the city in which I grew up — both in the sense that they are more in my thoughts, and because we visit them more regularly than when I lived in the southeast of England. The literal movement further away has produced its counter movements; and the most sustained period I have spent in Liverpool since going to university in 1971 also occurred after I'd started teaching in Japan: the period of convalescence after my operation in 1993 when I suffered a relapse and spent two weeks in a Liverpool pain control ward.

Moving on to Ghost Characters *then . . . I was looking at the bibliography on your website and noticed that there were quite a few poems which were listed as 'scheduled for* Ghost Characters' *but which don't appear in the book, suggesting that it's evolved quite a lot on the way to publication. Is that fairly typical when it comes to putting something like this together? How does a book come together? And how do you tell when it's complete?*

Your question about the poems slated for *Ghost Characters* is very much to the point. I'd forgotten what it says in that section of the website . . . Well, you'll find, I think, that the missing poems are all in the last section of *Selected Poems*. I wanted Carcanet to do the full collection, reprinting the last part of the *Selected*; but when Michael Schmidt found himself disinclined to take any more of my poetry, I had to leave those poems there and try to publish the rest where I could. In my ideal *Collected Poems*, the true *Ghost Characters* is the Shoestring collection, plus the last section of the *Selected* with the poems in three sections interspersed, in the right places, among the Shoestring order. That whole phase of work began as a gathering of poems in no particular order and with no 'theme' (something I'd rarely been able, or felt inclined to do); but then the suicide that forms the occasion of the second section happened — probably after I already had the title for the poem 'Ghost Characters' — and what I had been doing was interrupted by those poems, which I wrote fairly compulsively. The third section takes up the thread of the first by attempting a kind of echo effect, or at least that's the idea. The third part returns to the theme of both personal and cultural change. It was being written around the end of the century — a period that already feels antique, I fear.

When you say you wrote the poems in the second section 'fairly compulsively', does that mean they were all written in 'one go', as it were — not on the same day, obviously, but without working on other poems in between? And if so, is that quite unusual for you?

They were written, including the related ones in *Selected Poems* ('Equivocal Isle', 'All Around', 'An Air', and 'Apropos of Nothing') between mid October 1999 and May 2000. When they started suggesting themselves I was mystified about what had happened, and just found my thoughts turning to it over and over again. That's what I mean by 'compulsively'. So experiences of my immediate surroundings were inflected with that sorry event; and I was writing the poems speculatively to try and explain the confused feelings of regret, anger, and sorrow to myself. And, yes, I don't think I was writing much in the way of other poems at the same time. I was obsessed with that experience of understanding, remembering, and composing.

With these poems, in particular, I found reading them reminded me that the line between being 'forgivably curious' (as you put it in 'Exchange Values' elsewhere in the book) and unforgivably prurient is very thin. (I caught myself, for example, wanting to know 'the gist of it'— and not feeling comfortable about that— before I reached the poem called that). I suppose the inevitable comparisons — and contrasts — are with the poems in the second section of This Other Life *about a rape. Both sets of poems seem to enact a dilemma about what can and can't be said: what, perhaps, does discretion mean?*

That's the comparison I would make, and have made, myself. Discretion may well be the better part of valour, but not unequivocally in art. There are so many things we are not supposed to talk about, and they tend to be the things we most need to know how to understand properly. With those poems too the reader is placed in an uneasy relationship to the material, because that is what the writer is naturally both feeling, dramatizing, and, I hope, overcoming. My involvement with the events in these poems about a suicide is more indirect than in the poems about the rape. Yet both sets of poems negotiate similar dilemmas, which can also mean that they may veer between articulating a little too little and a little too much — with the aim of providing an experience which is not unlike what coming to understand something about another person's life might be. Perhaps it's also true that since the speaker of the poems takes on the dilemma, then readers are accompanied through it and, to this end, permitted the feeling that the issue of what's forgivable or unforgivable can be explored and thought about, while being only fictively suffered.

As a title Ghost Characters *seems to be an especially apposite and evocative one, given the themes and tones of much of the book . . . perhaps it would be useful to ask what 'ghost characters' are and where you came across the term?*

I got it from a book about Shakespeare as a reviser. Ghost characters are figures that are named in the *dramatis personae* of old plays, but who, for whatever reason, don't actually show up in the play itself. The title poem, which was called 'North Beach' in its earliest drafts was really brought to life by this idea of people who are both in, and not in, our various dramas — whether because they are memories, good and bad, of people for those who have emigrated, or they are people you have divorced, or who have died . . . It was a phrase that focused some of the oddities of living life in a kind of spiritual exile, one in which you have half-escaped from some things, and have been pushed out of others, and one in which memories and elsewhere can often be far more real and present than the routines you are going through on a daily basis. The fact that the word 'characters' has a range of uses — from theatrical roles, through being a 'bit of a character', to Chinese written characters, also gave it a spur.

It seems apposite, I suppose, because of the poems about the past, death, a sense of unreality, 'foreignness', anonymity . . . On the surface it seems quite a bleak collection. Or, perhaps, 'wintry' would be closer to it?

That effect is largely produced by the suicide in the middle of it, I imagine — though also from the mere fact that Sendai is a much more regularly and consistently snowy and icy place than any other that I had lived in before. There were opportunities to write poems about trudging through snow and being more or less snowed in that I hadn't had occasion to before. Actually, I quite like winter. I like the way that the distances reappear when the leaves fall. So 'wintry' to me is not necessarily 'bleak'. As I say, the poems about the suicide were written through an autumn, winter, and spring. There's an attempt to fit them into the experiences of the changing seasons — though my favourite autumnal ones 'All Around' and 'Equivocal Isle' are in the *Selected Poems*, as is the last, set in May, 'Apropos of Nothing'.

The weather's always been a very strongly and precisely realized presence in your work, but that's probably more so again now in Ghost Characters *than in any book since . . . well,* More About The Weather. *Is that something you were conscious of?*

In Japan the seasons are both more marked than in Britain, and are also celebrated year in, year out, as they change. So I would probably say that the poetry written up to 1989 is 'more about the weather' than the Japan and Italy based poetry, where it's more about the seasons.

The main reason for asking about the weather, though, is that it brings up a couple of other questions, one of which is about metaphors. Because, while

142

it's tempting to read the weather conditions in each poem as a metaphorical forecast for what Adam Piette suggestively describes in that quote on the back of your Selected as 'the weather of the mind', there's also a sense that they're not to be trusted. They look like metaphors but they're actually more akin to Larkin's 'That vase' than Shelley's west wind?

My guess would be that they're not quite either of these. The figures of description which carry emotional or symbolic significance are more animated and breathing significance, even grammatically speaking, than the Larkin, but they are also held back from being theorized as humanly meaningful in themselves as in the Shelley. They are given meaning by an improvising kind of projection, which is recognized as such, and this recognition prevents them from swelling up into a world of staged symbolic meanings.

Maybe Hardy is a more illuminating comparison on that score?

He's a poet and novelist I read intensively when young, and that sort of reading suffuses you in unpredictable ways because it's so formative or self-confirming.

The other question relating to the weather is to do with painting, because one thing I've not come across much in writing about your work is how 'painterly' it is — those lines in 'Ghost Characters', for example, about marriage celebrations with the ships in the distance, or the opening of 'Parmese Days'. There's a distinctive sense of visual composition here.

James Lasdun noticed this in his review of my first book, and Neil Corcoran is said to be writing something on the topic for the *Companion* volume from Salt. I was a keen amateur painter until the brain tumour operation dried up the tear duct in my right eye. Again, it's not something I exactly do consciously; but it is where much day-to-day inspiration (and I don't only mean for poetry) comes from — simply taking in the look of things and then occasionally feeling impelled to render that look in a poem — usually as a way to getting something else from out of the evocation.

That process seems quite close to the surface in poems like 'Tsukihama' or 'The Flow', for example — how did they come to be written? What elements and inspirations feed into them?

As I must have said before, my idea of inspiration seems to be an experience, often a visual one, with an accompanying phrase appearing in my head. The phrase may be linking the visual or random experience with some other issue that's been bothering me; or it may be a phrase with to-be-explored implications that hints at a connection between this stray experience of environment and whatever it may come to signify. Both the poems you mention are set in Japan. 'The Flow', like 'Opera Season', is one of those echo-effect poems in which the phrase 'ghost characters' appears — in this case because the poem is set in the same circumstances as the sequence from the first section with that title, while 'Equivocal Isle', 'Tsukihama', and 'Surface Tension' are all poems prompted by the same place: Okumatsushima, a brief drive further up the coast from the more touristy Matsushima of Bashô fame. What the two poems you mention have in common is a sense of the fleeting nature of experience, and this is of course a traditional theme in Japanese art. They are recordings of vivid moments in which a strong sense of loss is also present — even if the exact nature of the loss is not easily identified and instead insinuates itself into the circumstances.

With these poems picking up on traditional themes, would you say that Japanese art is having more of an influence on your work now?

No, I don't really; but after seventeen years working in Japan many things about the place have come to be understood, appreciated, taken for granted, accommodated as best they can be, and so on. It's probably nothing more than that — but, on the other hand, the implications of this might be more far-reaching than I usually allow myself to think.

And related to the actual process of writing, you seem to be quite a fierce editor of your own work before it's published. Do you revise a lot before publication? Or does that vary from poem to poem? Do some appear 'whole' and others go through a number of drafts? Is there a typical 'biography' of a Peter Robinson poem?

None of them ever appears whole. There's usually some sort of germ, a few words, a phrase or two, an experience with a minimal implicit narrative shape . . . So some words will go into a notebook, and get half forgotten. Then I wake up one morning with an extra line, or a title, or a notion about where the germ might go. Sometimes, if I'm lucky and not too busy, I might sit down with a piece of paper or notebook page and scribble out patches of a complete draft. Other times, when I am busy, I have to note down a new bit that forms itself as I'm walking between train and office, or during a meeting, or whatever. A sense of obscure excitement, a duty to myself, a need to find out what the pressure is — these sorts of feelings concentrate my mind on the thing and help to make time for it to be completed. That can be a matter of a few drafts over a couple of hours, or sometimes a bewildering number of versions returned to for days, even months and years, usually because there's something not properly attuned about the shape it's taking. When I've got what seems like a full version of the poem, I write it in a 'neat' notebook and put a date on it. That version usually gets some red-ink revisions of a local and polishing kind. Then it gets left. Over the next days or weeks I reread at intervals and do minor revisions if it seems they need them. Some of those poems stay in the manuscript book. Others get typed up, usually with a few little changes. Then they get sent off to magazines. If they are rejected, I might have another tinker — nowadays less than I used to do. Then little changes can come in on proofs . . . though one of the poems in *Ghost Characters* was recast at that stage. I just try to get the poem sounding as right as I can as smartly as I can — but it often does take time, not least because that's how I like to think the poetry will find ways to develop.

More generally, and returning to that Adam Piette quotation, he describes your poetry as a 'gauge', a sort of barometer recording 'pressures', and, having also read your own aphorism from Untitled Deeds *— 'You can't expect a kettle letting off steam to produce a convincing analysis of why it's boiling' — is that, perhaps, a distinction between types of poetry which could be applied across the board?*

Well, I don't think I write to let off steam exactly; I try to pour out the boiling water and murmur hints about why in this particular situation it's so hot — which is to say that I would implicitly use it as some kind of distinction for types of poetry, or perhaps a way of pointing towards what the poems that I can write may be attempting to do. After all, my things are evidently driven by the ways that the rhythm and structure of poems can shape and interpret experiences. There's also a belief in them about the value of art, and being moved by art, so that the emotion in my work is not something reflected from life, but a thought-filled feeling produced by the poem itself

— something added to life by the process of evoking life, in other words. Actually, to go back to your question, I don't think immediate anger or other kinds of life-prompted eruptions of feeling are the whole source of my poetry. The process described above of waiting for the germ to filter through the sensibility, and then allowing the process of composition to take the work where it seems I am enabled to take it, pretty much leaves behind any residual letting off steam that I might or might not have needed to do.

With There are Avenues *and* Ghost Characters *published in 2006, are you already looking towards what follows?*

Right now I'm caught up in the production process for two books of Italian translations, *The Greener Meadow: Selected Poems of Luciano Erba* (Princeton) and *Selected Poetry and Prose of Vittorio Sereni* (Chicago), both due out in autumn 2006. Beyond them, things are a little hazy. There's talk of a collection of stories called *How We Laughed*, and if that comes about I would have to do some finishing and polishing. I do have a completed collection of more poems, which is with a publisher, but not yet contracted — a book I hope to publish during 2008 when Liverpool is the European City of Culture. There's a book called *The Sound Sense of Poetry: Reading Techniques* being written when I have a moment or two . . . There are three effectively completed typescripts that haven't found homes yet: my novel, *September in the Rain*, *Most of the Time: Selected Poems of Pierre Reverdy*, and *The Personal Art: Selected Essays*, and there are other typescripts in various states too. Moving back to Kyoto, and other disturbances — which does sound like a book title — has also prompted quite a few new poems. So, as you can see, I'm managing to keep myself active.

Notes on Interviewers

PETER CARPENTER is co-director of Worple Press. Shoestring Press published his fourth collection of poetry, *Catch*, in October 2006, and he also contributed to *London: City of Disappearances*, ed. Iain Sinclair, (Hamish Hamilton, 2006).

JANE DAVIES is the editor of *The Reader* magazine, founded with Sarah Coley in 1997 (www.thereader.co.uk). She also directs the work of The Reader Centre at the University of Liverpool, where her team runs projects to bring literature out of the University, and books to life.

NATE DORWARD is a freelance music critic specializing in jazz and editor of the avant-garde poetry magazine and press *The Gig*. He lives in Toronto with his wife and daughter, and has a website at www.ndorward.com.

MARCUS PERRYMAN is a technical translator, management consultant and vocational trainer. With Peter Robinson, he has translated and published poetry by Ungaretti, Sereni, Fortini, and Cucchi. He lives in Verona, Italy.

ALEX PESTELL is working for a DPhil at the University of Sussex on the poetry of Geoffrey Hill. He is editor of the Internet poetry magazine *Signals* (www.signalsmagazine.co.uk).

TOM PHILLIPS is a freelance writer living in Bristol. After a decade in local radio, he edited *The Venue*, the South West's *Time Out*. Four of his plays have been produced, and his poetry has been widely published in magazines and anthologies, and in a first collection, *Burning Omaha* (Firewater, 2003).

ADAM PIETTE is Professor in English Literature at the University of Sheffield. Author of *Remembering and the Sound of Words* and *Imagination at War*, his current project is on Cold War culture. He helped set up Glasgow's Edwin Morgan Centre for Creative Writing, and co-edited *The Salt Companion to Peter Robinson* (2006).

KATY PRICE is Lecturer in English and course leader for Creative & Professional Writing at Anglia Polytechnic University. She co-edited *The Salt Companion to Peter Robinson* (2006), and is completing a book on astronomy, sex and friendship in the 1920s, focusing on William Empson and Arthur Eddington.

IAN SANSOM is author of *The Truth About Babies* (2001), *Ring Road* (2004), and *The Mobile Library* detective series. He writes for *The London Review of Books* and *The New York Times*, and is a columnist for *The Guardian*.

TED SLADE (1939-2004) was the founder and editor of *The Poetry Kit*. His pamphlet collection, *The Last Arm Pointing*, appeared from Flarestack.

Printed in the United Kingdom by
Lightning Source UK Ltd., Milton Keynes
139822UK00001B/78/A